The 12 Steps for Adult Children

Friends in Recovery

RPI Publishing, Inc.

Published by
RPI Publishing, Inc.
P.O. Box 44
Curtis, WA 98538
(360)-245-3386

The Twelve Steps are reprinted with permission of Alcoholics Anonymous World Services, Inc. Permission to reprint and adapt the Twelve Steps does not mean that AA has reviewed or approved the contents of this publications, nor that AA agrees with the views expressed herein. AA is a program of recovery from alcoholism only—use of the Twelve Steps in connection with programs and activities which are patterned after AA, but which address other problems, does not imply otherwise.

For the purposes of this book, the word "alcohol" in Step One has been changed to read "addiction," and the word "alcoholics" in Step Twelve has been changed to read "others."

NOTICE: This book is designed to provide information regarding the subject matter covered. It is provided with the understanding that the publisher and author are not engaged in rendering individualized professional services. These processes and questions are intended for group or individual study, and not designed to be a substitute for one-to-one professional therapy when such help is necessary.

ISBN 0-941405-12-5   pbk

Printed in the United States of America

Revised Edition

· 10 9 8 7 6 ·

In memory of Richard, Edward, and the countless others
whose lives were a struggle with addiction,
and who never found a solution.

This book is especially dedicated
to those addicts, family members, and friends
who have found the courage
to seek recovery.

TABLE OF CONTENTS

Appendix One

Appendix Two

Appendix Three

IMPORTANT INFORMATION

This book is designed to provide information regarding the subject matter covered. It is provided with the understanding that the publisher and authors are not engaged in rendering individualized professional services.

Appendix One contains a suggested meeting format for group study and includes review questions for each step.

Appendix Three contains suggested read-aloud materials for during the meeting.

THE TWELVE STEPS OF ALCOHOLICS ANONYMOUS

1. We admitted we were powerless over alcohol—that our lives had become unmanageable.
2. Came to believe that a Power greater than ourselves could restore us to sanity.
3. Made a decision to turn our will and our lives over to the care of God *as we understood Him.*
4. Made a searching and fearless moral inventory of ourselves.
5. Admitted to God, to ourselves, and to another human being the exact nature of our wrongs.
6. Were entirely ready to have God remove all these defects of character.
7. Humbly asked Him to remove our shortcomings.
8. Made a list of all persons we had harmed, and became willing to make amends to them all.
9. Made direct amends to such people wherever possible, except when to do so would injure them or others.
10. Continued to take personal inventory and when we were wrong promptly admitted it.
11. Sought through prayer and meditation to improve our conscious contact with God, *as we understood Him,* praying only for knowledge of His will for us and the power to carry that out.
12. Having had a spiritual awakening as the result of these steps, we tried to carry this message to alcoholics, and to practice these principles in all our affairs.

HISTORY OF
THE TWELVE STEPS

Alcoholics Anonymous began on June 10, 1935, co-founded by William Griffith Wilson (Bill W.) and Dr. Robert Holbrook Smith (Dr. Bob). Wilson conceived the idea of Alcoholics Anonymous while he was hospitalized for excessive drinking in December of 1934. During his hospital stay, Wilson had a spiritual experience that removed his desire to drink. In the following months, he tried to persuade other alcoholics to stop drinking just as he had. Wilson found his first "convert" in Smith, who was willing to follow Wilson's method to find freedom from alcoholism. Four years later, Wilson and Smith published the book *Alcoholics Anonymous*, that contains the Twelve Steps and a spiritually based program of recovery for alcoholism.

THE OXFORD GROUP

Various sources influenced the formulation of AA's program, as developed and recorded by Wilson. Of these, the British-born Oxford Group movement and its American leader, Samuel Moor Shoemaker, Jr., contributed most significantly to the basis of Alcoholics Anonymous. Both Wilson and Smith attended the Oxford Group meetings and based much of the AA program on this framework.

In the 1920s and 1930s, the Oxford Group movement became a revolutionary answer to antireligious reaction following World War I. Aiming to rekindle living faith in a church gone stale with institutionalism, the Oxford Group declared itself an "organism" rather than an "organization."

Group members met in homes and hotels, mingling their faith with meals. Despite its freedom from institutional ties, the movement was distinctly ecclesiastical and looked to the church as its authority.

Dr. Frank N. D. Buchman is cited as the leader of the Oxford movement. The group had no organized board of officers, but relied instead on "God control" through men and women who had fully "surrendered" to God's will. Buchman emphasized the need to surrender to God for forgiveness and guidance and to confess one's sins to God and others. Oxford Group followers learned also to make restitution for wrongs done and to witness about their changed lives in order to help change others.

The Oxford Group's teachings rested on the following six basic assumptions:

1. Human beings are sinners.
2. Human beings can be changed.
3. Confession is a prerequisite to change.
4. The changed soul has direct access to God.
5. The age of miracles has returned.
6. Those who have been changed are to change others.[1]

In addition, Wilson incorporated into AA's philosophy the Oxford Group's five procedures, which were:

1. Giving to God.
2. Listening to God's direction.
3. Checking guidance.

---

[1] Cantril, Hadley, *The Psychology of Social Movements* (Huntington, NY: Robert E. Kruger, 1941), pp. 147–148.

4. Restitution.
5. Sharing, both confession and witness.[2]

EVOLUTION OF THE TWELVE STEPS

While trying to attract more followers to sobriety from 1935-1937, Smith and Wilson attended Oxford Group meetings in New York led by Samuel Moor Shoemaker, Jr. "It was from Sam Shoemaker that we absorbed most of the Twelve Steps of Alcoholics Anonymous, steps that express the heart of A.A.'s way of life," Wilson later recalled. "The early A.A. got its ideas of self-examination, acknowledgment of character defects, restitution for harm done, and working with others straight from the Oxford Group and directly from Sam Shoemaker, their former leader in America, and from nowhere else."[3]

2 Kurtz, Ernest, *Not God: A History of Alcoholics Anonymous* (Center City, MN: Hazelden Educational Materials, 1979) pp. 48–49.
3 *Alcoholics Anonymous Comes of Age* (New York: Alcoholics Anonymous World Services, Inc., 1957), p. 199.

PREFACE

Those of us who participated in the development of this material are recovering individuals. Our belief is that the Twelve Steps are important healing tools. We believe that if we regularly apply these tools to our lives, we open ourselves to the healing love of a power greater than ourselves. Our intention is to carry the message of the Twelve Steps to all hurting people.

This revised edition reflects the spiritual and emotional growth of its contributors. It is also an expression of their commitment to work their individual programs and apply the principles of the Twelve Steps to their daily lives. The foundation of each contributor's recovery process is his or her relationship with a loving Higher Power.

A central theme and assumption of this work is that healing is possible. To some degree or another, everyone can experience freedom from the damaging effects of a less-than-nurturing environment. The journey we are about to begin is intended to give us an opportunity to experience peaceful and productive living. Feelings of unworthiness, anxiety, and inferiority diminish and are replaced by spiritual strength and virtues. Focusing on a relationship with our Higher Power transforms our obsessive need for other people's approval. Our attention is, instead, captivated by the promise of a new and healthier way to live.

The Twelve Traditions of Alcoholics Anonymous stress personal anonymity as a vital element of one's recovery. As "Friends in Recovery," we have chosen to remain anonymous to pursue our own personal growth. We understand the importance of facing ourselves honestly and placing our confidence in our Higher Power. We offer these materials, not as an end in themselves, but as a means to developing a healthy relationship with a Higher Power whom we choose to call God, with others, and with oneself.

INTRODUCTION TO
REVISED EDITION

The revisions in this book are the result of the authors' continued growth and recommendations received from individuals using the book. It is through their willingness to share their experience of using the material that these changes are possible. Improvements in the text are a result of feedback from groups using this book.

The 12 Steps for Adult Children is a personal guide to understanding the spiritual power of the Twelve Steps. This material is primarily for adults whose childhoods were negatively affected by a less-than-nurturing environment. This environment often resulted when the adults responsible for care were influenced by substance abuse, emotional problems, or compulsive behaviors. The Twelve Steps offer a way to grow beyond the harmful effects of a troubled home environment. Since the founding of Alcoholics Anonymous in 1935, the Twelve Steps have become a way for millions of people to change the course of their lives.

Twelve-Step recovery is not a program sponsored by any religious group or entity. However, people using this program find it in harmony with their own spiritual beliefs. It has no official religious affiliation. It is, however, a program that helps us to rediscover and deepen the spiritual part of ourselves. We also realize through working the Twelve Steps that our spirituality is important. We learn to live our lives according to the guidance of our Higher Power. We realize that the void or despair we feel is the result of our ignoring or rejecting our relationship with our Higher Power.

The foundation for this book is the Twelve-Step process. This process has helped countless individuals recover from many forms of addictive, compulsive, or obsessive behavior. This book is also a tool for writing one's personal story of recovery. It brings together the tested wisdom and the proven effectiveness of Twelve-Step principles. The material encourages self-understanding and emphasizes the importance of relying upon a power greater than ourselves.

When used as intended, the steps are a profoundly powerful process for allowing God to heal damaged emotions. *The 12 Steps for Adult Children* is a spiritual tool that helps us regain balance and order, and leads us to improved health and increased happiness through a renewed relationship with our Higher Power.

The Twelve-Step process of recovery is a spiritual journey. It takes us from a life where we experience confusion and grief to a place of peace and serenity—one day at a time. Many changes will come over us, but they won't happen all at once. The process takes time and patience. Our Higher Power instills in us the strength of character that only comes as a result of surrendering to the relationship.

We may have many self-defeating habits or behaviors that need correcting. When looking at our inappropriate methods of relating to others, it is important to remember the ways in which these patterns began. Because of the chaotic conditions of our childhood, we developed behaviors that now sabotage and assault the successful management of our lives as adults. Having grown up in emotionally repressive families, we became accustomed to denying our pain and discomfort. Most of us found it necessary to shut down our feelings and keep everything locked inside. We learned that expressing our own wants and needs caused rejection. This rejection stimulated intense feelings of inadequacy, and often times drove us to excessive use of mood-altering chemicals.

In our present environments, we may have trouble freely expressing pain, fear, anger, or need. We repress our true feelings because we continue to view our environment the same as we did in childhood. When we openly express our needs, we risk rejection. In order to avoid rejection, many of us compensate for our repressed feelings by doing things to extremes. Our behavior may include preoccupation with relationships or our job. Or we may cover our true feelings through overwork, overeating, or abuse of mood-altering substances such as drugs and alcohol.

Working the steps with the help of a Higher Power enables us to acknowledge much of our negative or repressed nature. This process is similar to sunlight and shadow. When we stand in the sunlight, we see that we cast a shadow. In the same way, as we begin to work the steps and measure ourselves by our Higher Power's standards and principles, we see our need. This does not automatically relieve us of the consequences of our past behavior, but it does help us to begin the work of change and healing.

Diligently seeking our Higher Power's will for us and working the material in this book enables us to reexamine our relationship with God. This process helps us discover new ways in which our Higher Power can enhance the quality of our daily lives. We learn to look fearlessly at our "shadow"—that part of us that has been ignored for so long. With the help of our Higher Power we experience changes in our unwanted behaviors such as people pleasing, repressed anger, obsessive thinking, or inappropriate sexual behavior.

With the help of a power greater than ourselves, the Twelve-Steps can be a tool to relieve our suffering, fill our emptiness, and help us extend God's presence in our lives. This releases energy, love, and joy that are new to us. It is a program we follow at our own pace, in our own way. We walk this journey one step at a time, with God's help and with the support of others in the program. All we need is an open mind. Much of the work is done by our Higher Power working through us. If we work the steps faithfully, we notice improvements in ourselves: our awareness, our sensitivity, our ability to love and be free. Our spiritual and emotional growth may surprise us.

GOD BLESS YOU.

STARTING THE JOURNEY

This book provides a practical way to use the Twelve Steps as a recovery tool, and to fully integrate the steps as an ongoing part of our recovery journey. The book helps us to identify and deal with issues that are interfering with our lives. If we approach this work seriously, we will experience recovery that nurtures physical, emotional, and spiritual well-being.

If you are new to Twelve-Step support groups, it is important to use other resources to help identify more specific issues that pertain to you. Many anonymous Twelve-Step programs have meetings that are focused on issues of relationships, food, sex, alcohol, drugs, etc. Taking part in groups such as Al-Anon, Adult Children of Alcoholics, or Co-Dependents Anonymous broadens your understanding of recovery issues and exposes you to others who share similar problems. You learn more about your own issues and have a sounding board for matters that may arise in your life. We encourage you to read additional material relating to the issues that are problems for you. This increases your awareness and enhances your ability to participate in the process. The Self-Help Resources in Appendix Three will help you identify an appropriate program for you. Other resources are also available through your library or in the telephone directory under "social service organizations" or "crisis intervention."

The Twelve Steps are a spiritual journey that can be used as a way out of self-destructive behavior, and also as a laboratory in which to learn new behavior. The Twelve Steps provide an opportunity to experience feelings, talk openly with others, enjoy life one day at a time, and develop healthy relationships. Meeting together in a group can be a powerful and transforming process. Loneliness diminishes as friendships among group members develop. Individuals can learn to be close to others by giving as well as receiving comfort and support. Communication outside the meeting is a vital element in the recovery process. Use the telephone and other ways to socialize and support one another outside the regular meeting time.

Relationships formed in support groups are a source of many benefits and rewards. The experience of being in a support group creates an atmosphere in which healthy, family-type communications can develop. It is a safe environment where trust can be learned. The small family groups provide an arena for quality sharing in which family secrets no longer need to be hidden, and the process of loving self-parenting can begin.

Wherever possible, share your insights with someone you trust. Communicating your discoveries to a trusted person can work miracles in your recovery journey. You will have an opportunity to share with others who can provide support and encouragement. As you share with others and build new relationships during this journey, be aware that they are not there to give advice or to fix you. True healing comes from developing a relationship with your Higher Power.

Due to our early exposure to negative behavior, many inappropriate behaviors may appear normal to us (e.g., resentment, greed, sexual abuse, dishonesty, gluttony, envy, laziness). Negative feelings may also seem normal (e.g., self-pity, sadness, insecurity, worry, fear of rejection, fear of abandonment). As we progress through the steps, this habit of seeing negative feelings or behavior as normal will change. We will experience growth in all areas by an increased sense of self-worth and self-esteem. Therefore, honest feelings and thoughts need to be appreciated and encouraged. This makes it possible to air elements of discouragement or distress before they hinder the group's progress.

Don't be discouraged if Steps One, Two, and Three seem overwhelming to you—this is a common reaction for persons who are new to the steps. Completion of these three steps forms the foundation for working the program. Allow sufficient time to go through the process of thinking about the questions and exercises. Do a little each day. This may take several days, a week, or longer. Be patient with yourself. Allow ample time to consider the contents and reflect on the meaning of each step. Impatience can seriously impair your effectiveness.

It is likely you will go through these steps more than one time. The program is a lifelong process to be used regularly, in part or in whole. At some point you may want to consider participating in a group that uses *The Twelve Steps—A Way Out,* a workbook that applies questions and exercises to the materials in this book. This book should not be your only involvement. It is just one part of working the Twelve Steps.

The material used in this book is a framework upon which our own life experiences can be reviewed with love and courage. We realize we have reached this point knowing very little about ourselves. As we develop a deeper relationship with our Higher Power, more will be revealed to us. Slowly we will be given the strength to put the past behind us and build a new life. Our lives can be less complicated if we work the steps regularly and continue to improve our relationship with our Higher Power. When we do this, our lives are blessed with the ongoing gift of peace and serenity.

Working the Steps is something that only we can do. Any attempt by another person to do our work or find answers for us inhibits our own recovery and limits our ability to become strong.

The process of working the Steps can be compared to the transformation of a caterpillar into a butterfly. The caterpillar is not clear that it is going to be a butterfly. Each part of its death and rebirth in the cocoon must be experienced.

The story is told of a man who noticed a cocoon on a bush in his yard. As he started to remove it from the bush and throw it away, he noticed the end was opening and a butterfly was struggling to escape. In an effort to help the emerging butterfly, he took it inside and carefully cut the cocoon away with a razor blade. The butterfly feebly crawled away from the open cocoon and, within a few hours, died. It needed the strength it would have gained from the struggle to free itself in order to survive in the outside world.

WORKING WITH
A RECOVERY PARTNER

A recovery partner is similar to a mentor or sponsor. This person can be a role model for learning how to enjoy a better quality of life through the love of a Higher Power and the wisdom of the program. It is important to choose someone who displays qualities you value and respect. These qualities can include:

- Belief in a Higher Power and a willingness to share his or her experiences with that Higher Power.

- Sincerity and honesty in sharing personal stories of recovery and how the Twelve Steps work in his or her life.

- Willingness to provide support and encouragement by listening and giving honest feedback without trying to force change.

- Ability to confront difficult issues and ask for accountability in keeping commitments.

- Openness of communication in all matters, even when discussing sensitive issues such as sexual abuse, violence, or other severe trauma-inducing subjects.

When choosing a recovery partner, it is advisable to select an individual who:

- Shares common interests and experiences and displays positive results in recovery.

- Understands and identifies with addictive, compulsive, or obsessive behavior.

- Has patience and compassion and is willing to listen attentively and offer suggestions without giving advice.
- Is available to spend time together when it is necessary.
- Is the same sex and can relate to personal issues in a nonthreatening way.

Questions arise when choosing a recovery partner. Some of them are:

- *What about the fear of rejection?* The process of dealing with fear of rejection can occur when asking someone to be a recovery partner. Because the program encourages rigorous honesty, we should begin by honestly telling the other person about any discomfort we feel when seeking a recovery partnership. We should offer the other person freedom of choice in the decision, and then detach from the outcome by trusting that our Higher Power's will prevails.

- *What happens when you are asked to be a partner and don't want to be?* This program can help us establish boundaries for ourselves. Boundaries include how we spend our time, express our feelings, and enter new relationships. Knowing when to say, "Thank you for asking, but that won't work for me," is all a part of setting boundaries. Setting boundaries can be an important step we take in simplifying our life, and does not require an explanation.

- *What about ending a recovery partnership?* Ending a recovery-partner relationship is part of learning when to select more appropriate support. It is also a reminder that one may not meet the needs of the recovery partner forever. Personal growth is a natural part of the process. The outcome may still be a very good friendship.

BENEFITS OF A RECOVERY PARTNER

Many benefits result from working with a recovery partner. Some of them are:

- Partners provide a non-threatening system of mutual accountability. For example, a partner can agree to call the other for support and prayer in abstaining from a harmful habit.

- Partners focus on each other's specific area of need each time they meet. Openly sharing thoughts and feelings helps to clarify needs in problem areas. This contributes to one's freedom from the past. The focus is to live honestly in the present with realistic expectations.

- Partners encourage one another to progress from a state of physical, emotional, and spiritual sickness to wholeness of life. It is normal to feel discomfort when unhealthy familiar behaviors are being transformed. Healthy behavior is a result of doing our Higher Power's will.

- Partners aid one another by being sensitive to personal and relationship needs. When partners openly share their faults with one another, honesty, trust, and healing occur. It is not appropriate to focus on a particular behavior and lose the value of the moment or the point of what is shared.

MUTUAL AGREEMENT
BETWEEN RECOVERY PARTNERS

A key part in establishing a relationship with a recovery partner is to agree on how the partners want to interact with one another. The agreement can establish:

- What the expectations are between one another.

7

- The length of time in which the agreement will be in effect.

- Specified times to evaluate the quality of the relationship.

- An understanding of how the relationship or agreement can be ended.

The agreement encourages the partners to make a sincere effort to:

- *Focus on the Twelve Steps as a tool to enhance one's relationship with God and others.*

At times encouragement or confrontation is needed when one has stopped working the steps. If a partner is unavailable or can't answer a question, seek out other Twelve-Step fellow travelers to help in understanding how they use this discipline in their recovery. It is inappropriate to impose personal views on one's recovery partner, particularly regarding one's relationship with God.

- *Be available for phone calls or meeting in person.*

A key to success in recovery is making and keeping commitments. Making a commitment to being available may be something new, but it is an important part of the process. Healing and change are easier when someone is available to offer support and encouragement.

- *Share their true feelings with their recovery partner.*

Rigorous honesty is important when sharing feelings. Healing is supported when partners tell the truth. Feelings require acknowledgment and appropriate expression without their being judged as right or wrong. Selective disclosure when talking about feelings may create doubt between partners.

- *Respect confidentiality and refrain from gossip.*

This program is built on trust. Fear of gossip may prevent some people from honestly sharing their pain. Healing will be hindered unless there is trust that personal matters between partners will remain confidential.

- *Accept discomfort as part of the healing process, and be willing to talk about it.*

Some meetings may be painful when memories of certain events or hurtful feelings are recalled. It is important to have a recovery partner available to show compassion and be supportive as we confront painful issues that cause us discomfort. It is best to admit the discomfort and deal with it. A recovery partner can help us face with the issues without reverting to old coping methods.

- *Support one another by listening attentively and offering constructive feedback.*

Listening attentively and offering feedback enables us to explore options and possible courses of action. This can strengthen one another's ability to make healthy choices that provide good results. Feedback, however, must not be confused with unsolicited advice.

- *Refrain from over-spiritualizing or intellectualizing when sharing.*

Partners are not spiritual directors to each other nor are they sources of advice in areas more appropriately handled by clergy or professional therapists. Instead, partners share their own experience, strength, and hope with one another. In spiritual matters, recovery partners share how God works in their life without over-spiritualizing or preaching.

- *Spend a minimum of 15 minutes each day reading Scripture, praying, and meditating, including prayer for your recovery partner.*

Prayer is talking to God, meditation is listening to God. Spending time in prayer and meditation can be a vital part of the recovery process. This is a spiritual program founded upon seeking to know God's will and experiencing His grace.

FINAL THOUGHTS

It is important to be tolerant and accepting of our recovery partner and others. This does not mean condoning addictive behavior slips or the rationalizations that follow. Being able to detach with love means not taking the behavior breakdown as a personal affront that one has somehow failed the recovery partner.

Partners are not responsible for each other. Their responsibility is to listen and respond from their own experience, strength, and hope. Having a trusted person who listens to us is helpful when working through the decision-making process. For many of us, having a recovery partner may be a way to experience the unconditional love of God for the first time.

COMMON BEHAVIOR
CHARACTERISTICS

Adults who were reared in troubled homes share certain common behavior characteristics. This is especially true when their caretakers were chemically dependent or emotionally repressed individuals. The behaviors reveal an underlying structure of disorder that is damaging to those involved. Although the general population displays many of the behaviors, individuals from troubled families tend to have a higher incidence of these characteristics. This list is intended to help you recognize areas of your life in which problem behavior characteristics are present. Examples are given to help you identify some of your thoughts, feelings, and behaviors.

- *We have feelings of low self-esteem that cause us to judge ourselves and others without mercy. We cover up or compensate by trying to be perfect, take responsibility for others, attempt to control the outcome of unpredictable events, get angry when things don't go our way, or gossip instead of confronting an issue. For example:*

  - I'm inclined to talk about my family and extended family. I often recite all of their faults and shortcomings to others.

  - When I am alone with my own thoughts I tend to criticize myself. Sometimes I feel stupid, inadequate, ugly, or worthless.

  - I don't feel important. I try to help others and hope they will notice me.

- I gossip and complain about those who make me feel powerless.

■ *We tend to isolate ourselves and to feel uneasy around other people, especially authority figures. For example:*

  - I like to blend into the scenery at work. I don't want the boss to notice me.

  - I feel uncomfortable in most conversations, especially when the focus is on me.

  - When I speak with someone in authority, I have trouble expressing myself.

  - I isolate myself because it's easier than dealing with others.

■ *We are approval seekers and will do anything to make people like us. We are extremely loyal even in the face of evidence that suggests loyalty is undeserved. For example:*

  - I offer to do favors for people even before they ask.

  - I worry about what others are thinking and saying about me. When people stop talking as I approach, I assume they're talking about me.

  - Although I may not like my boss or friends, I am loyal because I fear being rejected.

  - I find it hard to admit that I came from a troubled home. I feel guilty for admitting that my parents were less than perfect.

■ *We are intimidated by angry people and personal criticism. This causes us to feel anxious and overly sensitive. For example:*

  - I find it nearly impossible to listen to a harsh or critical speech.

- When someone with strong opinions speaks to me, I rarely share my true feelings. Instead, I say what I think the other person wants to hear.

- I may harbor a secret desire to retaliate against the angry and opinionated people who threaten my peace.

- I panic when someone points out a mistake or a problem with my work.

- *We habitually choose to have relationships with emotionally unavailable people with addictive personalities. We are less attracted to healthy, caring people. For example:*

  - I am in a relationship with someone who seems uncaring. I sense that my problems don't matter.

  - Life is always a crisis. I wonder what it would be like to live a normal life.

  - Others, not myself, seem to set the agenda for my life.

  - I sometimes feel that I deserve to "give in" to temptation, especially after I've suffered and done so much for others.

- *We live life as victims and are attracted to other victims in our love and friendship relationships. We confuse love with pity and tend to "love" people we can pity and rescue. For example:*

  - I seem to get the short end of every stick, and I agree with the saying, "No good deed goes unpunished."

  - I almost feel good about myself when I am doing something for others. However, I've learned from experience that they won't appreciate it.

  - My friends tell me that I am a good listener, but I resent how they lose interest when I share.

  - I spend a lot of my time fixing other people's problems.

- *We are either overly responsible or very irresponsible. We try to solve others' problems or expect others to be responsible for us. This enables us to avoid looking closely at our own behavior. For example:*

  - I am called when family members have a problem.

  - No one at my job or home cares as much or works as hard as I do.

  - When things fail at home or at work, I feel that I have somehow failed.

  OR

  - Others don't understand how sick I am, and I'm expected to do too much.

  - I'm just waiting for the right opportunity to become reinvolved in life.

  - I'm waiting for positive changes to happen in my life.

- *We feel guilty when we stand up for ourselves or act assertively. We give in to others instead of taking care of ourselves. For example:*

  - After I stand up for myself, I feel guilty and think maybe I was wrong.

  - When I feel safe with a close friend or family member, I share all my resentments about the pushy people in my life.

  - I feel sick when certain people want to see me or talk to me.

  - I store a great deal of anger inside instead of releasing it properly. I sometimes scream, slam doors, or break things when no one is around.

- *We deny, minimize, or repress our feelings from our traumatic childhoods. We have difficulty expressing our feelings and are unaware of the impact this has on our lives. For example:*

- There are portions of my childhood that I simply cannot remember.

- I sometimes react with overwhelming panic, anxiety, or fear in certain situations, and I have no idea why.

- I find it hard to get excited about things. Other people are annoyed when I don't share their excitement.

- When I start to feel too much anxiety or fear or when I hear the committee in my head, I look for something to distract me or kill the pain.

- *We are dependent personalities who are terrified of rejection or abandonment. We tend to stay in jobs or relationships that are harmful to us. Our fears can either stop us from ending hurtful relationships or prevent us from entering healthy, rewarding ones. For example:*

  - When someone close to me is silent or emotionally absent, I panic and fear the worst.

  - If my superiors don't recognize my work, I assume that they are displeased and ready to let me go.

  - When I disagree with a friend or companion, I later fear that I have irreparably damaged the relationship. I may even call several times to smooth things over or apologize.

  - I daydream about what it would be like to have a different job, spouse, friends, etc.

- *Denial, isolation, control, and misplaced guilt are symptoms of family problems. Because of these behaviors, we feel hopeless and helpless. For example:*

  - I just wish that people would leave me alone.

  - I try to manage my own life, but circumstances are always invading my plan.

  - I work hard to reveal little about myself, or I try to manage how people think of me.

- I don't have much hope that things will change. Good things happen to others, but not me. I seem to be cursed, or something.
- Sometimes I can't wait to go home, close the door, and disconnect from reality.

■ **We have difficulty with intimate relationships. We feel insecure and lack trust in others. We don't have clearly defined boundaries and become enmeshed with our partner's needs and emotions. For example:**

- If someone close to me is angry, I immediately feel threatened, even if the anger is toward another person or outside force.
- I can have sex with my spouse, but sometimes it is difficult to feel close or romantic.
- I often belittle my looks (if only to myself) or doubt my attractiveness.
- I may try to change my spouse or companion's mood by suggesting some pleasurable activity.

■ **We have difficulty following projects through from beginning to end. For example:**

- I finish most projects at the last minute.
- My desk is full of great projects that I *was* excited about but never handled.
- I have at least one room in my house that I hope no one ever sees.
- I feel guilty when I think of the time I've wasted on half-baked ideas or schemes.

■ **We have a strong need to be in control. We overreact to change over which we have no control. For example:**

- I want to know what my spouse or children are doing. I may even search their belongings.

- If others work for me, I find it hard to let them express their creativity. I want things done my way.

- When serious things happen that are beyond my control, I panic and take out my frustration on others. Or I take control through a flurry of activity.

- I find it hard to relax or sleep. People tell me that I am "high-strung."

■ *We tend to be impulsive. We take action before considering alternative behaviors or possible consequences. For example:*

- I settle for less than what I really want, because I find it hard to decide.

- I sometimes write and mail letters that I later wish I could get back.

- I go places and do things without planning. I have made many "mistakes" in life.

- I make commitments that I later regret. I may even ask my spouse or children to call and cancel appointments for me.

We admitted we were powerless over the effects of addiction—that our lives had become unmanageable.

Understanding Step One

When we were young, we were sometimes tickled by those who were bigger than us. They would often tickle us so hard and long that we lost control. We would gasp and cry for them to stop, and we would scream, "I quit, I give up, please stop!" Sometimes they stopped when we cried and sometimes they stopped only when someone older or bigger came to our rescue.

Step One is like this episode from childhood. Our own life and behavior is like the cruel tickler who inflicts pain and discomfort. We have done this to ourselves. We took control to protect ourselves, but results have frequently ended in chaos. And now we don't want to give up control and release ourselves from the torment. In Step One we admit that we can't stand it anymore. We plead for release. We cry, "I quit!"

Working Step One

Step One is an opportunity to face reality and admit that our life isn't working with us in control. We embrace our powerlessness, we stop pretending. In a sense, we stop the juggling act that we have performed for so long. We admit that we can't continue the illusion of control. If it means that all the balls fall to the ground, then so be it. We are so tired of juggling our lives, we are ready to accept whatever comes.

Preparing for Step One

The way we manage our own lives brings us to the end of our rope. We hit bottom. Our ways and our efforts fail us. At this point, Step One provides needed direction for our unmanageability. We prepare ourselves by realizing that Step One is the first step in a journey toward wholeness. This step stops us. It puts a halt to our own efforts and gives us permission to quit.

Prayer for Step One

To Be Honest, God

To be honest, I'm not sure who I'm praying to.Maybe I'm talking to myself, but...

To be honest, I can't take any more.My life is a failure, I feel like a...

To be honest, I want to die, I want to quit,I want to quit hurting me, I want to quit hurting them.

To be honest, I don't know what to do. For the first time, I'm really lost...

To be honest, I don't know if anyone hears me,But if someone hears, please come find me.

(Taken from *12 Step Prayers for A Way Out*, pages 5-6)

The ideas presented in Step One are overwhelming to most of us until we begin to see our lives as they really are. It is threatening to imagine that we could be powerless; that our lives could be unmanageable. Our life experiences remind us that our behavior does not always produce peace and serenity. Our background, if affected by alcohol or other types of family problems, undermines our best plans, desires, and dreams. Often, our troubled background has caused us to lose touch with ourselves. Our lives are full of unwelcome behaviors and overwhelming emotions.

We live in a culture that places a high value on individual accomplishment. Most of us, from the time we were small children, were bombarded by the ideal of high achievement. Being competitive in school, sports, and business is viewed as important in our society. We are taught that if we compete hard enough we will be "winners" and, therefore, good people. If, however, we don't measure up to what is expected of us and are losers, we believe we are failures. Due to the absence of good role models during childhood, many of us are confused. We don't know where we fit in. We continue to allow our worth and self-esteem to be determined by what we do and what others think of us. Looking back at our past, we may continue to classify ourselves as losers. We may condition ourselves to fail. Our low self-esteem keeps us from becoming winners and causes extreme stress and anxiety.

As we mature, matters get worse. Our stressful lives give us no satisfaction, and the stress compounds our problems. Our fears and insecurities increase, creating a sense of panic. Some of us revert to abusing mood-altering substances such as drugs, alcohol, or food to relieve our tension. In more subtle ways, we may bury ourselves in school activities, work, relationships, or other addictive/compulsive behaviors to combat the anxieties that seem to overwhelm us. When we come to grips with ourselves and realize that our lives are just one big roller-coaster ride, we are ready for Step One. We have no alternative but to admit that we are powerless and that our lives have become unmanageable. When we reach this point, it is important that we seek help.

Step One forms the foundation for working the other steps. In this vital encounter with the circumstances of our lives, we admit our powerlessness and accept the unmanageability of our lives. Surrendering to this idea is not an easy thing to do. Although our behavior has caused us nothing but stress and pain, it is difficult to let go and trust that things will work out well. We may experience confusion, drowsiness, sadness, sleeplessness, or turmoil. These are normal responses to the severe inner struggles we are experiencing. It is important to remember that surrender requires great mental and emotional energy as well as determination. Do not give up. A new life of freedom awaits us.

PERSONAL REFLECTION

In Step One, we come to grips with the reality of our lives. Perhaps for the first time, we finally admit defeat and recognize that we need help. In looking at Step One, we see it has two distinct parts. The first part is the admission that we have obsessive traits. Those traits appear in the way we try to manipulate the affairs of our lives to ease the inner pain that results from our struggles. We are in the grip of an addictive process that has rendered us powerless over our behavior. The second part is the admission that our lives have been, and will continue to be, unmanageable if we insist on living by our own will.

Our pride cries out against the idea of powerlessness and giving up control. We are accustomed to accepting full responsibility for all that happens in our lives and in the lives of others. Having grown up in a troubled environment, it is natural for us to react. Some of us become overly responsible while others withdraw and become very irresponsible. Until we reach an intolerable threshold of pain, we will be unable to take the first step toward liberation and renewed strength. We must realize that before we can totally surrender.

As we begin to accept the reality of our condition, we naturally reach out to others for answers. We feel like timid spiritual beginners and wonder why the quality of life we are seeking has escaped us. Friends may tell us to see a therapist or talk with a favorite relative. No matter how many outside sources we seek, there will be no relief for us until we, by ourselves, in our own minds and hearts, acknowledge our powerlessness. Then, and only then, will we begin to see that Step One is the beginning of a way out.

Step One is an ongoing commitment. We must remember that our damaging traits, habits, and behaviors are a part of us. They are unconscious reactions to the stresses of life. As we notice self-defeating behaviors and reactions surface, we can admit our powerlessness and seek help from a Higher Power. This simple act opens the door to the healing change we seek.

The second part of Step One, admitting that our lives are unmanageable, is as difficult as acknowledging that we are powerless. We can become more observant of the thoughts and behaviors we still rely upon from our past as a way to hide the truth about ourselves today. We need to be totally honest, drop the disguises, and see things as they really are. When we stop finding excuses for our behavior, we will have taken the first step toward achieving the humility we need to accept spiritual guidance. It is through this spiritual guidance that we can begin to rebuild ourselves and our lives.

A physical disease can only begin to be healed when we acknowledge its presence. In a similar way, the spiritual healing of our obsessive/compulsive behavior begins when we acknowledge the problem behavior. Until we realize this truth, our progress toward recovery will be blocked. Our healing begins when we are willing to acknowledge our problems and take the necessary steps to resolve them.

As we progress through the steps, we will discover that true and lasting change does not happen by trying to alter our life conditions. Although it is tempting to think so, outside adjustments cannot correct inside problems. Extraordinary healing requires surrendering the belief that we can heal our lives by manipulating our environment. Our willingness to work the steps will enable us to begin our true healing, which starts on the inside.

KEY IDEAS

Powerless: In Step One we discover that recovery begins with an admission that we are powerless. We admit that we do not have the power on our own to live life as our Higher Power intends.

Unmanageable: We have tried to manage our lives and the lives of others. However, our management has always met with failure. In Step One we admit that we cannot control or manage our lives any longer.

STEP TWO

Came to believe that a power greater than ourselves could restore us to sanity.

Understanding Step Two

"I looked at the white, turbulent waters of the river and melted inside. Any courage I had mustered seeped through my sweating pores. My legs turned to spaghetti at the thought of taking the inflated raft down the rapids—all in the name of fun. Then the river guide, who would steer and command our raft, began to speak. He sounded so sure of himself, so confident that everything would be fine. He gave us instructions, taught us the commands, made us laugh, and even put me at ease. It was crazy, I guess, but I trusted him to make this insane river ride a safe and enjoyable experience."

Step Two is about faith—trust and believing. Faith isn't intellectualized—it just is. Faith isn't manufactured—it's from a power greater than ourselves. Faith isn't earned—it's a gift. Faith isn't optional—it's a must. Many turbulent and troubled waters await us in our recovery. When we finally look to a Higher Power, we will already have the faith to believe that a Higher Power exists.

Working Step Two

Step One, if worked properly, leaves us feeling empty. We have admitted our own powerlessness and the unmanageability of our lives. So we are left saying, "If I am powerless and cannot manage my life, who can?" God can! God helps us by putting a simple seed of faith in our hearts. That seed of faith is not great. It is simply a growing confidence that someone else, far greater than ourselves, will take charge. Step Two helps us acknowledge the seed of faith given to us by our Higher Power. This begins the process of trusting that a power greater than ourselves is at work in our lives.

Preparing for Step Two

We prepare for Step Two by acknowledging that we don't know everything about our Higher Power. Many of us have a distorted view of God. Although we are not quick to admit it, we may believe that God is like our abusive or absent parents or significant others. We may believe that God doesn't care how we feel, that God is cruel and waiting to judge us. We may have been threatened with God's punishment all our lives.

Preparing for Step Two requires that we set aside our old images and mistaken beliefs about God. For now we can simply hold on to the words of AA's Second Tradition, "...there is but one ultimate authority—a loving God..."

Prayer for Step Two

Greater Than Myself

Higher Power,
The sky over my head,
The generations that came before,
The stars that shine above,
The world and its creatures,
The body in which I live, *is greater than I ??*
How so?
The air I breathe,
The order and way of the universe,
All these things are greater than I am.
Who am I to doubt you God?

(Taken from *12 Step Prayers for A Way Out,* page 13-14)

With the help of Step One we came to grips with the fact that we are powerless and our lives are unmanageable. Our next step is to acknowledge the existence of a power greater than ourselves. Believing in God does not always mean that we accept God's power. In Step Two, we begin to reestablish our relationship, or, establish a relationship with our Higher Power for the first time. This step gives us an opportunity to experience faith in a power greater than ourselves. This connection will grow and become a vital part of our daily lives.

For many of us, this step presents major obstacles. Since we find it hard to trust others, the loneliness of our present condition causes us to fall back on our own resources. We may even doubt that a Higher Power can heal us or even be interested in doing so. Unless we let go of our distrust and begin to lean on God, we will continue to operate in an insane manner. The chaos and confusion of our lives will only increase.

Depending on our religious background, some of us may have been taught that God is an authority to be feared. We never saw God as a loving Higher Power. As children, we were anxious and feared doing something wrong. Sometimes the threat of being punished by God was used by adults to control our childish behavior. Our fear of displeasing God magnified our growing sense of guilt and shame. As adults, we continue to fear people in authority and are often overcome by guilt and shame for simple misdeeds.

We still may be harboring childhood anger because we felt that God disappointed us. Due to the severity of our experiences, some of us rejected God because trusting in God did not relieve our pain. Despite our belief that there is a Higher Power with us, in moments of fear we sometimes doubt this. Even those who are dealing with their problems and are in contact with their Higher Power experience periodic moments of doubt and fear. In Step Two, our goal is to believe that God, a power greater than ourselves, can guide us in our journey toward peace and healing.

For some of us, belief in self-will and our ability to manage our own lives is all we have. We perceive God as a crutch for children and weak-willed individuals who are incapable of managing their own lives. As we begin to see God's true nature, a weight is lifted from our shoulders. We begin to view life from a different perspective.

Step Two is often referred to as "The Hope Step." It gives us new hope as we begin to see that help is available to us. We must simply reach out and accept what our Higher Power has to offer. In Step Two we form the foundation for growth of our spiritual life, which will help us become the person we want to be. All we need to do is be willing to believe that a power greater than ourselves is waiting to help us.

PERSONAL REFLECTION

Coming to believe in a power greater than ourselves requires faith. In the past, we have placed our faith in our own abilities to run our lives, and that faith has proven worthless. It never did for us what we thought it would. Now we need to place our faith in a power greater than ourselves. At first, it may seem unrealistic to place our faith in a power we cannot see or touch. Step Two provides a foundation for the spiritual development that will help us achieve a greater sense of personal fulfillment.

As newcomers, we often encounter stumbling blocks with this Step. One obstacle is the difficulty we have in believing that a power greater than ourselves exists. Although we may be aware of many examples in which "faith as small as a mustard seed" has worked wonders in the lives of others, we may doubt that it could apply to us. We could be resisting the idea of a Higher Power's healing presence. We may find it impossible to imagine that, through "believing," the intensity of our obsessions and compulsions could decrease. In time, our faith begins to grow as we recognize that even the most devout, spiritually grounded persons suffer moments of doubt.

Before entering a twelve-step program, many of us strongly resisted spiritual concepts and beliefs. We neither understood spirituality, nor felt it had anything to offer us. Our longing for the nurturing and caring parent limited our ability to understand the concept of a trusting and loving Higher Power. Perhaps we felt that our prayers were unanswered. Our faith may have been shattered by our belief that, if God exists, it is not a loving God. Often, our low self-esteem created the feeling that we were not worthy of the attention of care of a Higher Power, or that it could even exist.

Our traumatic childhood experiences caused us to become defiant, indifferent, resentful, self-deluded, and self-centered. Our adult lives need to be restored to a more balanced state. We can find that balance if we are willing to believe that a power greater than ourselves can restore us to sanity. When we attempt to do it alone, we often deceive ourselves by looking to outside sources for the causes of our problems. With the help of a Higher Power, these deceitful behaviors can be healed from the inside out.

One way God helps us see our condition clearly is to bring us into contact with others who share experiences similar to ours. It becomes evident, when sharing our stories in meetings and through fellowship, that each of us can maintain "emotional sobriety" only one day at a time. Also, our Higher Power helps us realize that actions destructive to ourselves or to others are not acceptable. As we become more dependent on God's power, the quality of our lives will improve.

When we started this program, we may have been expecting instant results. From our childhood, we remember feeling anger or confusion when things didn't happen "right now." In this program, sudden change is the exception, not the rule. It requires patience and perseverance to achieve the peace of mind we seek. Each of us is unique. Recovery begins for each of us at different stages in the steps. Some may experience instant relief, whereas others may not begin to feel stronger until later in the program. There is no set rule or guideline. Progress occurs at the appropriate time.

During the initial stages of accepting the presence of a Higher Power, it is sometimes helpful to be consciously aware of the special occurrences around us. We can view coincidences in our lives as small miracles, gifts or simply interventions of our Higher Power. By taking the time to thank our Higher Power for simple things like "not getting a ticket for running a red light," or "receiving an unexpected call from someone we are thinking about," we learn to accept a Higher Power. Our willingness to express gratitude to this Power assists us as we "come to believe."

When we are ready to accept our powerlessness and unmanageability (Step One), and when we trust our Higher Power to restore us to sanity (Step Two), we will be ready to make a decision to turn our lives over to the care of God (Step Three). There is no need to rush the process of working the steps. We move forward in faith so we will be able to proceed with the remaining steps. The faith we develop in Step Two is our most important building block in recovery. Our success in the program depends upon our relationship with our Higher Power and our belief that this power can help us.

Coming to believe in a Higher Power and admitting we behave in a destructive manner require a great deal of humility. Our previous lack of humility contributed greatly to our past ineffectiveness. As we work toward a more balanced lifestyle, we see the importance of humility in all our affairs. Our growth is considerably enhanced by our willingness to be humble and accept our humanness. As we attend meetings and work the Steps, we discover the peace and serenity possible through surrendering our self-will and humbly seeking to improve the quality of our lives.

KEY IDEAS

Higher Power: Because Step One has helped us understand our powerlessness, we need a power beyond ourselves to help and heal us. Our Higher Power does not have to be precisely identified or named. Our Higher Power may not be anything like the God we were taught about in earlier religious training. Our Higher Power, who will nurture and carry us through our recovery, will be revealed in divine power, presence, and help according to our unique needs. All we really need to know about our Higher Power now is what AA's Second Tradition says, "...there is but one ultimate authority—a loving God...." The emphasis is on the word "loving." The God of this program is a loving and nurturing power, who has our best interests in mind.

Belief: Belief in something or someone requires more than acknowledging that something or someone exists. It requires trust and commitment. It is one thing to believe that a chair will hold my weight. It is another thing to sit in it. When I sit in the chair, I truly believe in it. In Step Two we come to believe that a power greater than ourselves can restore us to sanity. We do more than acknowledge God's existence—we begin to exercise trust that God will hold us.

STEP THREE

Made a decision to turn our will and our lives over to the care of God as we understood God.

Understanding Step Three

Imagine the insanity of trying to perform surgery on ourselves. At the first hint of pain from the scalpel, we would stop. Healing would never happen. It is just as insane to think that we can manage our own recovery. We must put our lives into the hands of our Higher Power, who knows the extent of our disease. Our Higher Power alone knows what is needed for healing and has our best interest at heart.

In Step Three we decide to turn the scalpel over to God as we understand God. We decide to turn over control of our will and our lives. We have admitted our powerlessness and inability to manage our lives. We also have come to believe that God can heal us, and now, we decide to turn our will and our lives over to God's care.

Working Step Three

We work Step Three by going through a decision-making process, similar to other big decisions we have made in our lives. For example, when making a decision about buying a car, we consider such things about the car as cost, color, condition, etc. We also take into consideration things about ourselves such as our ability to pay, transportation needs, personal preferences, etc. Finally, when all things have been weighed, we make a decision. In a similar way we work Step Three. We consider how well the present management of our lives is going. We consider our needs, our ability, the future. We take time to contemplate the changes. And finally, we make a decision that our Higher Power is the only one able to manage our lives, that our Higher Power's plan for us is best.

Preparing for Step Three

We prepare for Step Three by thoroughly doing Steps One and Two. If we are not convinced that we are powerless and that our lives are unmanageable, we are not ready for Step Three. This step will be difficult if we have not come to believe that a power greater than ourselves can restore us to sanity and is able to care for us. We also prepare for Step Three by fully accepting our powerlessness and our inability to manage our lives. We prepare by allowing God to plant seeds of faith in our hearts. When those things are in place, Step Three comes easily.

Prayer for Step Three

My First Prayer

I surrender to you my entire life,
O God of my understanding.
I have made a mess of it trying to run it myself.
You take it, the whole thing, and run it for me,
According to your will and plan.

(Taken from *12 Step Prayers for A Way Out*, page 23)

Step Three is the central theme of all the steps. It is the point at which we make a decision to turn our will and our lives over to the care of God as we understand God. It is an important cornerstone for building an effective and peaceful life. In Steps One and Two we established the basis for turning our lives over to God's care. The commitment in Step Three must be repeated more than once, as we are just beginning to turn things over to our Higher Power. Repeated working of the first three steps helps to build a solid foundation for working the total program.

Many of us come to this program with strong negative perceptions about the world in which we live. Those perceptions may be based on hurtful childhood experiences, misguided academic training, or simply the accumulated lessons of our lives. We may have perceived God to be unloving and judgmental. If we experienced violence as children, we may find it hard to trust. Whatever the source, our recovery is hindered if our beliefs make it difficult to let go of our fear and surrender our lives to God. In Step Three, we decide to take a leap of faith and put our lives in his hands.

Until now, our perceptions of reality have led us into many obsessive\compulsive behaviors. Admitting our responsibility for these behaviors is often too difficult. It implies that we have not been "good people." Denial is our only recourse, and acts as a shield against facing ourselves as we really are. When denial is at work, it is like a shuttered window, closing out the sunlight. In Step Three, we begin to open the shutters and allow our Higher Power's light to enter. It gives us a source of light with which we can examine our behavior and understand reality.

Step Three is an affirmative step. It is time to make a decision. In the first two steps, we became aware of our condition and accepted the idea of a power greater than ourselves. Although we began to know and trust our Higher Power, we may find it difficult to surrender total control of our lives. However, if the alternative is to face the loss of people or things vital to our lives, such as family, job, health, or sanity, guidance of a Higher Power might be easier to accept. Our lives may have many relationships that are being ruined by our behavior. Rather then being discouraged by these discoveries, we can use them to prompt our surrender to a power greater than ourselves.

As we begin to allow God's will to act in our lives, our self-destructive tendencies become fewer and much less distracting. Often, the confusion and grief we cause ourselves and others prevent us from successfully working and practicing the steps. Making the decision to begin this journey is an act of great importance and should not be made in a time of emotional upheaval. The key elements in Step Three are making the decision with a clear and rational mind, being committed to that decision, and, finally, trusting the outcome to our Higher Power.

As we surrender our lives and stop carrying the burdens of our past, we will begin to feel better about ourselves. The more we learn to trust in our Higher Power, the more we will trust ourselves and others. Our decision to choose God's way will restore us to the fullness of life. As we free ourselves from our self-will, we in turn free ourselves from much of our negative behaviors, and we are able to deal more effectively with the daily routine of our lives. Our impatience and irritability disappear as we come to know our Higher Power's love and yearn to share it with others. Our lives include peace and serenity, and we become the persons we were meant to be.

PERSONAL REFLECTION

In Step Three, we acknowledge our need for guidance, and make the decision to surrender our lives to God's care. Our Higher Power becomes our new manager, and we accept life on God's terms. We discover a way to live that is free from the emotional pollution of our past, allowing us to enjoy new and wonderful experiences. Step Three provides us with an opportunity to turn away from behavior that fosters addiction, discouragement, sickness, and fear.

Many of us begin the Step Three process by deciding to turn over only certain parts of our lives. We are willing to surrender the most difficult problems when we see they are making our lives unmanageable. We cling to other areas of our lives because we think we can manage them or because we think they are necessary for our survival. We eventually realize that we cannot barter with God. We must be prepared to surrender our entire will and every part of our lives to his care if we want to recover. When we are truly able to accept this fact, our journey to wholeness has begun.

Step Three may make us feel we are losing our identity. We may think we are going to lose everything. Not knowing what is going to happen is frightening. Most of us have tried desperately to control our environment. Many of these behavior traits were developed during childhood and came about as a direct result of the circumstances in which we were raised. Deep within us may be a fearful childhood memory and a trembling child anxious about someone's anger, criticism, threats, or violence. As children, we tried to fix or take care of the people around us so they would not abandon us, leaving us with only broken promises and shattered dreams.

The conditions in which we were raised often kept us from ever trusting in God. Our prayers may have been unanswered, and we could not imagine how a loving God could be so cruel to us. Step Three is an opportunity to start over. As we work the Steps, we will get in touch with memories of childhood hurts. We also will begin to experience our Higher Power's healing love, and repair the damage that has been done. Then we can look forward to a return of childlike spontaneity, and a growing capacity to give and receive love and nurturing.

Learning to trust in a Higher Power and accept support will enhance the quality of our lives. We will no longer feel the need to carry our burdens by ourselves. Much of the pain of our past is a result of feeling totally alone. Our need to control people and events kept us isolated, but as we trust and surrender, we will begin to relate better with others. With God's presence, our sense of self-esteem will improve, and we will begin to recognize that we are worthwhile human beings. Our capacity to receive and give love will increase, and we will come to place great value on fellowship and sharing.

The Twelve Steps is a spiritual program—a tool for healing. Step Three is an opportunity to let a power greater than ourselves take charge of our lives. This liberates us from the pressure of feeling responsible for everything and everyone, or expecting someone else to take responsibility for us. As we surrender to our Higher Power, we develop a feeling of peace and serenity in our lives.

It is not important to understand how our Higher Power works in order to "let go." We need only to believe in the process. If we have trouble working Step Three, it is probably because we are having difficulty with the "belief" aspect of Step Two. In this case, we need to return to Step Two before going further.

When we experience meaningful results in working Step Three, a change comes over us. We are calmer and feel that a weight has been lifted from our shoulders. It can happen suddenly or gradually, as we consciously accept the guidance resulting from our partnership with a Higher Power. If we experience a feeling of euphoria, it will not last forever. At times, we might revert to our old behavior patterns. At this point, we need only to recognize this. There are no saints in the program—we all have "slips". However, as we work the steps daily, we become more willing and able to turn our lives over consistently.

There is a paradox in the way this program works. The less we try to manage our own lives, the more effective we become. When we give up managing our own lives and trust in our Higher Power's plan for us, we find we are calmer and more accepting of things around us. Friends may compliment us on how well we are managing our lives. As we stop trying to restrict ourselves to a course of rigid self-discipline, people may recognize how at ease we are in simply being ourselves.

Most of us start this journey in an effort to stop repeating painful cycles of ineffective and behavior. We are usually in search of answers to complex questions of life. Some of us may have experimented with lifestyles and beliefs that appeared to offer solutions. We may have been looking for a relationship with a Higher Power that transcended things of this world. This life-giving experience is available through the Twelve Steps.

KEY IDEAS

Turn it Over: This phrase of surrender is a key idea for Step Three. Imagine turning over your car keys to someone else. Think of turning over a job or a responsibility to a more capable person. People who have been in the program for any length of time talk about turning over problems and daily troubles to their Higher Power. For those of us who are working Step Three for the first time, we are turning over our will and our lives to God's care. Whatever imagery you choose, let the meaning always be the same: the surrender of your will and life. Turn it over. Give God control.

Self-Will: Self-will is the determination within us all to control our own lives. Self-will in itself is not wrong; God has given us the power to choose. The problem with choice occurs when our will conflicts with God's. Our choices have brought us pain, hardships, addictions, compulsions, and self-defeating behaviors. God's will for our lives brings us hope, healing, and peace. His plans are good. Our self-will is best exercised in choosing surrender to God.

STEP FOUR

Made a searching and fearless moral inventory of ourselves.

Understanding Step Four

If we lived alone and were unable to see, we would be faced with a number of special needs. For example, we might find it difficult to clean our home thoroughly by ourselves. We might ask a sighted friend to come over and help. This friend would see areas in need of cleaning that we had missed. Our friend would point these problems out and then, we hope, help us clean them.

In Step Four we realize there are areas of our lives that need attention. We also realize that we cannot see all those areas. Denial has kept us blinded to the dirt in our corners. Low self-esteem has kept us ignorant about the beauty and worth of our lives. In this step, our Higher Power comes to us as a caring friend. God opens our eyes to the weaknesses in our lives that need changing and helps us to build on our strengths.

Working Step Four

Just as any business takes inventory of its stock, we take inventory of our lives in Step Four. With clipboard in hand, we walk down the aisles of our lives and note areas of weakness and strength. When we come to relationships, we take stock of the resentments and grudges, and also examine our loving and healthy relationships. When we come to communication, we note the lies, but we also list the positive ways we share with others. In this process we can ask for help from our Higher Power, who knows the contents of our warehouse far better than we do.

Preparing for Step Four

We prepare for Step Four by recognizing that denial has been operating in our lives. We prepare by asking our Higher Power for the courage to face those areas that have been protected by denial. And we prepare for Step Four by planning to nurture ourselves during and after the inventory process. The goal of nurturing is to support ourselves to assure a thorough inventory and our continued progress. Our need for nurturing should not be under estimated. The Twelve-Step process is not easy, and Step Four is particularly demanding.

Prayer for Step Four

Light a Candle

O God of my understanding,
Light a candle within my heart,
That I may see what is therein
And remove the wreckage of the past.

(Taken from *12 Step Prayers for A Way Out,* page 33)

Step Four begins the growth steps of our journey. Here, we examine our behavior and expand our understanding of ourselves. The adventure of self-discovery begins with Step Four and continues through Step Seven. During these next four steps, we will prepare a personal inventory, share it with others in the program, and invite God to remove our shortcomings. Being totally honest in preparing our inventory is vital to the self-discovery that forms the foundation of our recovery. It allows us to remove obstacles that have prevented us from knowing ourselves and truthfully acknowledging our deepest feelings.

Step Four helps us get in touch with our "shadow," that part of us that we have hidden away for so long—our repressed nature. In the process of making our inventory, we will develop and broaden our understanding of our behavior. We will see that our "shadow" is an integral part of our nature and must be accepted by us. This part of our nature hides our resentments, fears, and other repressed feelings. As we begin to see ourselves, we will learn to accept our whole character—the good and the bad. This acceptance will free us to discover survival behaviors that began in childhood. In the context of our turbulent early years, these behaviors were lifesaving. However, their continuation into our adulthood renders us dysfunctional.

Denial is a key survival skill that we learned early in childhood. It stunted our emotional growth by keeping us in a make-believe world. We often fantasized that our situation was better than it really was. Denial protected us from our feelings and helped us repress the pain of our family environment. Our shame and guilt caused us to be silent, rather than to be honest and face the fear of being ridiculed by others. This withdrawal hindered us from developing into mature, emotionally healthy adults. As our self-discovery unfolds, we begin to recognize the role that denial has played in our lives. This realization is the basis for our acceptance of the truth of our personal history.

Resentment and fear are two issues that need to be dealt with before we can begin the process of preparing our inventory. Our resentment toward people, places, and things that have injured us keeps us preoccupied and limits our ability to live in the present. Resentment results from hiding the bitter hurts that have tarnished our lives. It evokes anger, frustration, and depression. When our resentments are unresolved, we risk developing physical and mental illnesses.

Fear limits our ability to be rational. When fear is present, it is difficult to see situations in their true perspective. Fear is the root of other repressive and painful feelings. It prevents us from expressing ourselves honestly and stops us from responding in appropriate ways to threatening situations. So to change our behavior, we must first face and accept our fears. By acknowledging our fearful nature, we can expect a temporary loss of self-esteem; fortunately, this will return as we become more willing to rely on our Higher Power.

Preparing our inventory requires that we look to our Higher Power for guidance. We renewed our relationship with our Higher Power in Steps Two and Three, and now we ask God for help. We will look closely at our personal histories and acknowledge what we see in them. As the process unfolds, we will recognize the need for change. This task will be much easier if we just remember that God is with us. With God's help, we can courageously review our strengths and our weaknesses.

Step Four gives us the opportunity to recognize that certain skills, acquired in childhood, may be inappropriate in our adult lives. Blaming others for our misfortunes, denying responsibility for hurtful behavior, and resisting the truth are behavior patterns we must discard. These behaviors were developed early in life and have become character defects. Our willingness to be honest about what we uncover will give us the clarity of mind that is vital for our continued recovery.

Putting our thoughts on paper is valuable and necessary when completing Step Four. The process of writing focuses our wandering thoughts and allows us to concentrate on what is really happening. It often causes repressed feelings to surface and gives us a deeper understanding of ourselves and our behavior. Our fearless moral inventory provides insights regarding our strengths and weaknesses. Instead of judging ourselves, we need to accept whatever we discover, knowing that this discovery is merely another step toward a healthier life. We must be honest and thorough to complete Step Four successfully.

PERSONAL REFLECTION

Denial stems from our childhood environment, which we were unable to control. This was our way of dealing with the confusion, instability, and violence of the adults around us. We rationalized what was happening and invented acceptable reasons for their unacceptable behavior. By doing this, we ignored the chaos and denied the overwhelming problems. As we matured, our denial continued to protect us from the need to face reality and helped us hide behind our delusions and fantasies.

Denial was one of the many ways we protected ourselves as children. It has many faces and can be easily masked. It appears in different ways and operates in various fashions. Some recognizable forms are:

- *Simple Denial:* To pretend that something does not exist when it really does (e.g., discounting physical symptoms that may suggest the presence of problems).

- *Minimizing:* To acknowledge a problem, but refuse to see its severity (e.g., admitting to an overusage of prescription drugs when in fact there is overt addiction).

- *Blaming:* To recognize the problem, then blame someone else for its cause (e.g., blaming others for your tendency to isolate).

- *Excusing:* To offer excuses, alibis, justifications, and other explanations for our own or others' behavior (e.g., calling in sick for a partner when the actual cause of the absence is drunkenness).

- **Generalizing:** To deal with problems on a general level which typically avoids personal and emotional awareness of the situation or conditions (e.g., sympathizing with a friend's unemployment when you know the underlying cause is irresponsibility).

- **Dodging:** To change the subject to avoid threatening topics (e.g., talking about the weather when your spouse is discussing the overdrawn checkbook).

- **Attacking:** To become angry and irritable when reference is made to the existing condition, thus avoiding the issue (e.g., arguing about work conditions when the boss addresses tardiness).

Taking a personal inventory is similar to cleaning a closet. We take stock of what we have, examine what we want to save, and discard what is no longer useful. It doesn't have to be done all at once, but it must be done eventually. If we take small sections at a time, the cleaning is more thorough and the long-term results are better. In the same way that clothes can trigger memories of the past, our inventory may provoke both positive and negative memories. The past is history, and there is no need to dwell on it. This reflection of the past is only a tool to help us understand our current behavior patterns. Our main concern now is for our future.

In Step Four, we will get in touch with many behaviors and attitudes that have been with us since childhood. Our growing awareness about the way we were raised will help us understand that our present behaviors are the result of our need to survive in an environment over which we had no control. As adults, we now can choose a different lifestyle for ourselves. We can learn to conduct ourselves in a way that is nurturing to us. As we look at our strengths and weaknesses, we will become aware of the areas of our lives that need to be strengthened. We also will see those areas in which we exhibit strength through our wise choices. We can use the inventory to decide which areas of our lives need changing, and which areas seem to the way we want them to be.

Our next task is to look at resentment and recognize how damaging it is to us. It is the number one offender and often the major cause of spiritual disease. As we list our resentments, we see how they have affected our self-esteem, our well-being, and our personal relationships. Holding on to resentment causes stress, anxiety, and uncontrollable feelings of anger. If these are unresolved, serious emotional and physical consequences will develop. If we allow our resentments to prevail, we unknowingly give them the power to influence our lives. Serious depression can develop and ultimately destroy our lives.

The second most destructive offender is fear. It is the emotion we most strongly feel when we begin to look at ourselves. When fear is present, our need to deny, ignore, and avoid reality is increased. Our unrealistic perspective becomes greatly exaggerated and intensifies our emotional responses. Fear can cause us tremendous pain. It attacks us physically and causes feelings that range from apprehension to panic. When fear is present, we may become nervous, nauseated, or disoriented. As we inventory our fears, we may discover that they are a direct result of our inability to make decisions. Or we may believe that if we could make the right decisions, things would be different. And some of the most troubling decisions directly relate to the boundaries we know must be established. Fear is the first response we feel when we aren't in control of our lives. It is the opposite of faith. When we fear, we feel loss of control and we doubt God's ability to help.

Facing our resentments and fears requires a great deal of courage. Our past tendency has been to shut down our feelings. Now we begin to look at areas of our lives that we have never explored before. It is important to realize that God is with us and will help us every step of our way. With God's help and understanding, the pain will diminish.

As part of preparing our Step Four inventory, we will look at our character traits and examine our strengths and weaknesses. Our strengths appear in behavior that has positive effects on us as well as on others. Our weaknesses are revealed in behavior that is destructive to ourselves and others. Before we can correct our problem areas, we need to acknowledge and examine both. Understanding begins when we discover how we became the people we are—how we formulated the ideas, beliefs, and attitudes that govern how we act. This doesn't require years of therapy.It involves only an honest consideration of the forces, influences, and needs that developed our survival skills and molded our current character traits.

When preparing our inventory, we may encounter some difficulties. If we are blocked at some point, denial may be operating. We need to stop for a moment, reflect on what we are attempting to do, and analyze our feelings. We must also ask God for help. In times like this, God's presence means a great deal to us, and we must be willing to look to God for support.

The inventory we are preparing is for our own benefit, not the benefit of others. It will help us make a major breakthrough in our self-acceptance and lead us further along the road to recovery. As we go to Steps Five, Six, and Seven, the process continues to unfold as we acknowledge the truth about ourselves, discuss it with others, and, finally, ask God to remove our shortcomings. For now, our goal is to concentrate on making an honest and thorough inventory. If done properly and sincerely, our Step Four work will help us break free from the bondage of our past.

KEY IDEAS

Moral Inventory: A moral inventory is a list of our weaknesses and our strengths. In this text the weaknesses are also referred to as wrongs, character defects, faults, and shortcomings. This inventory is something we thoughtfully accomplish with our Higher Power's help. It is for our own benefit.

Survival Skills: Survival skills are those familiar defenses that we developed to protect ourselves from the chaos of our childhood homes. These early childhood survival skills followed us into adult life and added to our struggles.

Denial: Denial is a key survival skill. We protect ourselves by not admitting that anything is wrong. We ignore the real problems by replacing them with a host of elaborate explanations, rationalizations, and distractions such as minimizing, blaming, excusing, dodging, attacking, etc.

Resentment: Resentment is a major roadblock to recovery that must be removed. Resentment is the bitterness and anger we feel toward those whom we perceive as threats to our security or well-being or those who have caused us harm. If not removed, our resentments hinder our progress and growth.

Fear: Fear is often our first response to anything new. We meet change with fear because we feel threatened by so many things. Fear creates a physical response that begins with the release of adrenaline and ends up with the whole body on alert. This alerted state often leads to persistent and unwanted tension and can develop into stress-related illness.

Shadow: Although "shadow" may sound odd or unfamiliar, the idea of a battle between light and dark is reality. The idea of darkness and shadow illustrates the evil side of this world and the corrupt nature in ourselves. "Shadow" refers to the darkness we carry within us. Just as our shadow follows our every move, our dark side is always with us. Our shadow is most evident when contrasted with the light of day.

IMPORTANT GUIDELINES IN PREPARING YOUR INVENTORY

The materials offered in this Step Four Inventory Guide are different from the inventory guides used in other Twelve-Step programs. They emphasize those feelings and behaviors most commonly seen in individuals from homes where substance abuse or other damage-inducing behavior was prevalent. When preparing your inventory, choose the traits that specifically apply to you. Don't tackle them all at once. For now, only work on the ones that you feel comfortable doing. Come back to the difficult ones later. Focus on recent events and record words and actions as accurately as possible. Take your time. It's better to be thorough with some than incomplete with all.

The inventory begins with resentment and fear, followed by a series of feelings and behaviors to be examined. This process prepares you for Step Five. You are the primary beneficiary of your honesty and thoroughness in this inventory. It is important to refrain from generalizing. Be as specific as possible.

Following the section on character weaknesses there is an opportunity to list your character strengths. This chapter also includes an "Additional Inventory" for you to record your weaknesses and strengths that were not listed in the text.

NOTE: Step Ten includes a special inventory to measure the progress you have made since your initial inventory in Step Four.

RESENTMENT

Resentment is an underlying cause of many forms of spiritual disease. Our mental and physical ills are frequently the direct result of this unhealthy condition. No doubt others have harmed us, and we have a legitimate right to feel resentful. However, resentment doesn't punish anyone but ourselves. We can't hold resentments and find healing at the same time. It's best released by asking God for the strength to forgive the offender. Learning to deal with resentment in a healthy way is an important part of our recovery process.

When we resent, we may be:

Feeling injured   Feeling left out
Experiencing low self-worth   Feeling violated
Retaliating   Angry or bitter

Consider situations where resentment is a problem for you.

Example: *I resent* my boss *because* he doesn't care to hear my explanation of why I am depressed. *This affects* my self-esteem. *This activates* unexpressed anger. *This makes me feel* even more depressed.

Self-Evaluation: On a scale from one to ten, how much does resentment negatively affect your life? Number one indicates that it has little negative effect. Number ten indicates that it has great negative effect. Circle where you are today.

| 1 | 2 | 3 | 4 | 5 | 6 | 7 | 8 | 9 | 10 |

FEAR

Fear is an underlying cause of many forms of spiritual disease. It is the first response we feel when we aren't in control of a situation. A wide range of mental and physical ills are frequently the direct result of this unwholesome emotion. Fear often prevents us from seeing options to effectively resolve the issues causing the fear. Learning to acknowledge fear in a healthy way is an important part of our recovery process.

When we fear, we may be:

Feeling threatened   Resisting change
Experiencing rejection   Fighting for survival
Facing our mortality   Anticipating loss

Consider situations where fear is a problem for you.

Example: I *fear* my spouse *because* I feel that I am never able to please him/her. *This affects* my self-esteem and sexuality. *This activates* my fear of abandonment. *This makes me feel* worthless and angry.

Self-Evaluation: On a scale from one to ten, how much does fear negatively affect your life? Number one indicates that it has little negative effect. Number ten indicates that it has great negative effect. Circle where you are today.

| 1 | 2 | 3 | 4 | 5 | 6 | 7 | 8 | 9 | 10 |

REPRESSED OR INAPPROPRIATELY EXPRESSED ANGER

Anger is a major source of many problems in the lives of adults who were reared in chaotic homes. It is a feeling that we often suppress, because admitting it makes us uncomfortable. In our chaotic homes, the turmoil was so intense that we either denied our anger or expressed it inappropriately. We felt it was safer to protect ourselves and simply hoped our feelings would go away. We were not aware that repressed anger could lead to serious resentment and depression. It causes physical complications that can develop into stress-related illnesses. Denying anger or expressing it inappropriately causes problems in relationships because we cannot be truthful about our feelings and must always be pretending.

When we repress or inappropriately express anger, we may experience:

Resentment	Depression
Anxiety	Self-Pity
Jealousy	Stress

Consider situations where anger is a problem for you.

Example: *I inappropriately express anger* toward my son *because* I am embarrassed by his behavior. *This affects* my self-worth. *This activates* my fear of rejection. *This makes me feel* incompetent as a parent.

Self-Evaluation: On a scale from one to ten, how much does anger negatively affect your life? Number one indicates that it has little negative effect. Number ten indicates that it has great negative effect. Circle where you are today.

1	2	3	4	5	6	7	8	9	10

APPROVAL SEEKING

Many of us fear disapproval and criticism. As children, we desperately wanted to receive approval from our parents, grandparents, siblings, and significant others. This rarely occurred for most of us. As a result, we constantly sought validation. This continued into adulthood and seriously affected the way we pattern our lives and thinking around the needs of others. Rather than look for approval in a positive way, we seek validation in order to feel better about ourselves and get people to like us. This keeps us out of touch with our own feelings and desires, and prevents us from discovering our own wants and needs. We look for reactions in others, and attempt to manage their impression of us. We constantly strive to please everyone and often stay in relationships that are destructive to us.

When we need approval from others, we may be:

People pleasing   Feeling unworthy
Fearing failure   Ignoring our own needs
Fearing criticism   Lacking confidence

Consider situations where approval seeking is a problem for you.

Example: *I seek approval* from my friends *because* I want to feel better about myself. *This affects* my relationship with my friends. *This activates* my fear of rejection. *This makes me feel* like I'm not important to anyone.

Self-Evaluation: On a scale from one to ten, how much does approval seeking negatively affect your life? Number one indicates that it has little negative effect. Number ten indicates that it has great negative effect. Circle where you are today.

1	2	3	4	5	6	7	8	9	10

CARETAKING

As children, we frequently assumed the responsibility for concerns and problems of others that were far beyond our capability to handle. As a result, we were deprived of a normal childhood. The unrealistic demands placed on us, and the praise we received for being "little adults," made us believe we had Godlike powers. Taking care of others boosted our self-esteem and made us feel indispensable. It gave purpose to our lives. As caretakers, we are most comfortable with chaotic situations where others assure us that we are needed. Although we often resent others for taking and not giving, we are unable to allow others to care for us. We don't experience the joy of taking care of ourselves.

As caretakers, we may:

Be co-dependent	Lose our identity
Ignore our own needs	Rescue people
Feel very responsible	Feel indispensable

Consider situations where caretaking is a problem for you.

Example: *I take care of* my boyfriend's financial problems *because* I want him to love me more. *This affects* available funds for my own financial needs. *This activates* my resentment and tendency to withdraw. *This makes me feel* very lonely.

Self-Evaluation: On a scale from one to ten, how much does caretaking negatively affect your life? Number one indicates that it has little negative effect. Number ten indicates that it has great negative effect. Circle where you are today.

1	2	3	4	5	6	7	8	9	10

CONTROL

As children, we had little or no control over our environment or the events that took place in our lives. As adults, we have extraordinary needs to control our feelings and behavior, and we try to control the feelings and behavior of others. We become rigid and unable to have spontaneity in our lives. We trust only ourselves to complete a task or to handle a situation. We manipulate others in order to gain their approval and keep a balance of control that makes us feel safe. We fear that our lives will deteriorate if we give up our management position. We become stressed and anxious when our authority is threatened.

Due to our need to be in control, we may:

Overreact to change   Be judgmental and rigid
Fear failure   Lack trust
Manipulate others   Be intolerant

Consider situations where control is a problem for you.

Example: *I attempt to control* my nineteen-year-old son *because* I am afraid of losing him. *This affects* my communication with him. *This activates* my fear of abandonment. *This makes me feel* very frightened and powerless.

Self-Evaluation: On a scale from one to ten, how much does control negatively affect your life? Number one indicates that it has little negative effect. Number ten indicates that it has great negative effect. Circle where you are today.

| 1 | 2 | 3 | 4 | 5 | 6 | 7 | 8 | 9 | 10 |

FEAR OF ABANDONMENT

Fear of abandonment is a reaction to stress that we developed in early childhood. As children, we observed unpredictable behavior from responsible adults. We never knew from one day to the next if our parents would be there for us. Many of us were abandoned either physically or emotionally. As our parents' addictions increased in severity, their inability to parent also increased. As children, we simply were not important. As adults, we are inclined to choose partners with whom we can repeat this pattern. We try to be perfect by meeting all our partner's needs in order to avoid experiencing the pain of abandonment. Our need to reduce the possibility of abandonment takes precedence over dealing with issues or conflicts. This behavior produces a tense environment with poor communication.

When we fear abandonment, we may:

Feel insecure   Worry excessively
Become co-dependent   Become caretakers
Feel rejected   Avoid being alone

Consider situations where fear of abandonment is a problem for you.

Example: *I fear abandonment* by my husband *because* he doesn't pay much attention to me. *This affects* my peace of mind. *This activates* my caretaking and manipulation of him. *This makes me feel* very frightened and vulnerable.

Self-Evaluation: On a scale from one to ten, how much does fear of abandonment negatively affect your life? Number one indicates that it has little negative effect. Number ten indicates that it has great negative effect. Circle where you are today.

| 1 | 2 | 3 | 4 | 5 | 6 | 7 | 8 | 9 | 10 |

FEAR OF AUTHORITY FIGURES

Fear of people in roles of authority can be a result of our parents' unrealistic expectations of us—wanting us to be more than we were able to be. We see people in authority as having unrealistic expectations of us and thus, we fear we cannot meet their expectations. We are unable to deal with people whom we perceive as being in positions of power. Simple assertiveness displayed by others is often misinterpreted by us as anger. This can cause us to feel intimidated and to become over sensitive. No matter how competent we are, we compare ourselves to others and conclude that we are inadequate. As a result, we constantly compromise our integrity in order to avoid confrontation or criticism.

Fear of authority figures may cause us to:
Compare ourselves to others   Take things personally
Fear rejection   React rather than act
Feel inadequate   Be arrogant

Consider situations where fear of authority figures is a problem for you.

Example: I fear my boss *because* I don't want her to know how incompetent I feel. *This affects* my actions when I am around her. *This activates* my need to isolate—I try to be unnoticed. *This makes me feel* childish and immature.

Self-Evaluation: On a scale from one to ten, how much does fear of authority figures negatively affect your life? Number one indicates that it has little negative effect. Number ten indicates that it has great negative effect. Circle where you are today.

| 1 | 2 | 3 | 4 | 5 | 6 | 7 | 8 | 9 | 10 |

FROZEN FEELINGS

Many of us have difficulty expressing our feelings or even realizing that we have them. We harbor deep emotional pain and a sense of guilt and shame. As children, our feelings were met with disapproval, anger, and rejection. For survival purposes, we learned to hide our feelings or repress them entirely. As adults, we are not in touch with our feelings. We can only allow ourselves to have "acceptable" feelings to stay "safe." Our true nature is distorted so we can protect ourselves from the reality of what is truly happening. Distorted and repressed feelings cause resentment, anger, and depression, which often lead to physical illness.

When we have frozen feelings, we may:
Be unaware of our feelings   Be depressed
Have distorted feelings   Struggle with relationships
Become ill   Withhold conversation

Consider situations where frozen feelings are a problem for you.

Example: *I repress my feelings* toward my spouse *because* I don't want to be hurt. *This affects* my actions and limits my ability to communicate with my spouse. *This activates* my need to isolate and causes me to be accused of being insensitive and unaffectionate. *This makes me feel* very isolated and lonely.

Self-Evaluation: On a scale from one to ten, how much do frozen feelings negatively affect your life? Number one indicates that they have little negative effect. Number ten indicates that they have great negative effect. Circle where you are today.

| 1 | 2 | 3 | 4 | 5 | 6 | 7 | 8 | 9 | 10 |

IRRESPONSIBILITY

In childhood, life was so chaotic we felt that nothing we did mattered. The models we had were untrustworthy and irresponsible, so we didn't know what was normal. The expectations placed on us were beyond our ability to achieve. We couldn't be what everyone wanted us to be, so we quit trying. Rather than compete with successful siblings, we unplugged, we gave up. As adults we are irresponsible. We wait for things to change before we begin to take initiative. We believe life has been so unfair to us that we won't claim responsibility for our present condition. We are over-whelmed by our problems, but don't know how we can make a difference.

When we are irresponsible, we may:

Become detached	Feel like victims
Under-achieve	Appear uncaring
Expect others to take care of us	Have false pride

Consider situations where irresponsibility is a problem for you.

Example: *I behave irresponsibly* when too much is expected of me *because* I know that I can't do what my family wants. *This affects* my self-esteem. I want to isolate and hide. *This activates* my resentment and anger. I hate these people for expecting this of me. *This makes me feel* guilty and afraid.

Self-Evaluation: On a scale from one to ten, how much does irresponsibility negatively affect your life? Number one indicates that it has little negative effect. Number ten indicates that it has great negative effect. Circle where you are today.

| 1 | 2 | 3 | 4 | 5 | 6 | 7 | 8 | 9 | 10 |

ISOLATION

We usually find it safer to withdraw from surroundings that are uncomfortable for us. By isolating ourselves, we prevent others from seeing us as we really are. We tell ourselves that we are not worthy and, therefore, do not deserve love, attention, or acceptance. We also tell ourselves that we cannot be punished or hurt if we don't express our feelings. Rather than take risks, we choose to hide, thereby eliminating the need to face an uncertain outcome.

When we isolate ourselves, we may:

Fear rejection   Feel defeated
Procrastinate   Be timid and shy
Be lonely   See ourselves as different

Consider situations where isolation is a problem.

Example: *I isolate* from my spouse *because* he/she is so negative toward me. *This affects* my self-esteem. *This activates* my negative self-talk and anger. *This makes me feel* worthless and stupid.

Self-Evaluation: On a scale from one to ten, how much does isolation negatively affect your life? Number one indicates that it has little negative effect. Number ten indicates that it has great negative effect. Circle where you are today.

| 1 | 2 | 3 | 4 | 5 | 6 | 7 | 8 | 9 | 10 |

LOW   SELF-ESTEEM

Low self-esteem is rooted in our early childhood. During this time we were rarely encouraged to believe that we were adequate or important. Because of constant criticism, we believed that we were "bad" and the cause of many family problems. To feel accepted, we tried harder to please. The harder we tried, the more frustrated we became. Low self-esteem affects our ability to set and achieve goals. We are afraid to take risks. We feel responsible for things that go wrong, and when something goes right, we do not give ourselves credit. Instead, we feel undeserving and believe it is not going to last.

When we experience low self-esteem, we may:

Rescue or please others	Isolate from others
Be non-assertive	Have negative self-image
Appear inadequate	Fear failure

Consider situations where low self-esteem is a problem for you.

Example: *I feel low self-esteem* when I'm asked to speak in front of others *because* I believe everyone knows how worthless and unimportant I feel inside. *This affects* my ability to speak intelligently. I mumble, make excuses, and apologize for myself. *This activates* self-hatred and negative self-talk. I want to go hide afterward. *This makes me feel* hopeless.

Self-Evaluation: On a scale from one to ten, how much does low self-esteem negatively affect your life? Number one indicates that it has little negative effect. Number ten indicates that it has great negative effect. Circle where you are today.

1	2	3	4	5	6	7	8	9	10

OVERDEVELOPED SENSE OF RESPONSIBILITY

As children in a dysfunctional home, we felt responsible for our parents' problems. We tried to be "model children" and arrange things the way we thought others wanted them to be. We believed that we were responsible for the emotions and actions of others—even for the outcome of events. Today we remain supersensitive to the needs of others, and we try to assume responsibility for helping them get their needs met. It is important for us to be perfect. We volunteer to do things so people will appreciate us. Our sense of responsibility causes us to overcommit, and we have a tendency to take on more than we can handle effectively.

When we are too responsible, we may:

Take life too seriously	Over-achieve
Appear rigid	Be perfectionists
Manipulate others	Have false pride

Consider situations where overdeveloped sense of responsibility is a problem for you.

Example: *I feel overly responsible* when things aren't going well at work *because* I think it's my fault. *This affects* my health. I'm extremely tense and I get headaches. *This activates* my resentment and anger. I hate these people for letting me do all the work. *This makes me feel* guilty.

Self-Evaluation: On a scale from one to ten, how much does overdeveloped sense of responsibility negatively affect your life? Number one indicates that it has little negative effect. Number ten indicates that it has great negative effect. Circle where you are today.

| 1 | 2 | 3 | 4 | 5 | 6 | 7 | 8 | 9 | 10 |

INAPPROPRIATELY EXPRESSED SEXUALITY

We think of our sexual feelings as unnatural or abnormal. Because it is awkward to share our feelings with others, we have no opportunity to develop a healthy attitude about our own sexuality. As children, we may have explored our physical sexuality with peers and then been punished severely. The message was "sex is dirty, is not talked about, and is to be avoided." Some of us saw our parents as very disapproving or even as totally nonsexual beings. We may have been molested by a parent or close relative who was out of control. As a result, we are uncomfortable in our sexual roles. We do not freely discuss sex with our partners for fear of being misunderstood and abandoned. As parents, we may avoid discussing sexuality with our children and deny their need for developing a sexual identity.

Due to inappropriately expressed sexuality we may:

Lose our sense of morality	Be lustful
Seduce others	Be frigid or impotent
Avoid intimacy	Feel guilt and shame

Consider situations where sexuality is a problem for you.

Example: *I inappropriately express my sexuality* when my spouse wants intimacy *because* I feel dirty and unlovable. *This affects* our relationship. *This activates* my resentment and anger toward my spouse for not understanding, consequently I hate myself for being this way. *This makes me feel* lonely.

Self-Evaluation: On a scale from one to ten, how much does sexuality negatively affect your life? Number one indicates that it has little negative effect. Number ten indicates that it has great negative effect. Circle where you are today.

1	2	3	4	5	6	7	8	9	10

CHARACTER STRENGTHS

Consider the positive character strengths you already possess in the following areas:

Emotional: Healthy feelings or affective responses to one's self and others (e.g.,I am able to feel and express my love for my spouse and my children).

Spiritual: The good ways one relates to a Higher Power (e.g., I have a strong commitment to my Higher Power).

Relational: Positive and supportive interaction with others (e.g., I have a healthy friend-ship with Robert).

Moral: Proper ethics and behavior in thoughts and actions (e.g., I have a clear conscience concerning my business affairs).

Intellectual: Quality attention and energy devoted to mental activities (e.g., I devote time to reading and study).

Self-care/nurturing: Healthy concern and care for self (e.g., I take time to go fishing and do things for me).

ADDITIONAL INVENTORY

Take time now to consider the strengths and weaknesses that you did not consider in your Step Four inventory.

STEP FIVE

Admitted to God, to ourselves, and to another human being the exact nature of our wrongs.

Understanding Step Five

Imagine a house that had been shut up for several years. A blanket of dust covers everything. Signs of decay abound: cobwebs in strings like party decorations. Stuffy and stale odors of mildew and mold. Unrecognizable knickknacks on the dust-covered mantle. Forgotten and faded pictures on stained walls. Eerie feelings that hover like ghosts from years gone by. We can't wait to open all the doors, to pull back all the drapes, to vent the shut-up rooms. We turn on every light and expose each darkened, dusty corner. We watch the light of day sweep out the demons of darkness and shadow.

Our lives are like closed-up houses. All our shameful secrets, embarrassing behaviors, and spoiled hopes lie hidden from view. The air of our lives is stale because we have been afraid to open the doors and windows to anyone else lest we be found out, rejected, or shamed. Step Five is our emergence. When we admit the nature of our wrongs to God, ourselves, and another human being, we are opening the doors and windows of our lives. We are displaying our true selves.

Working Step Five

We work Step Five by bringing our Step Four inventory to our Higher Power in prayerful admission. We work Step Five by being honest with ourselves, by looking ourselves in the eye, and reciting our inventory. We work Step Five by sharing our inventory with someone we can trust, someone who will understand, someone who will encourage and not condemn us. The work of admitting our wrongs is the task here. Not easy work, but absolutely necessary.

Preparing for Step Five

We prepare for Step Five by scheduling an undistracted time with God and with ourselves. We prepare by prayerfully searching for another human being with whom to share. And we prepare by asking God for help in completing this step. Sometimes our tendency is to round off the edges and water down the truth of our inventory. Our Higher Power can give us the courage to be brutally honest about ourselves.

Prayer for Step Five

Give me Courage

God, I've never had to tell somebody else about my wrongs
I've never confessed to a priest or even to my dog,
I've kept it all inside and sought to hide.
I've been too frightened to admit what I really am.
Give me courage to tell somebody else what I've found.

(Taken from *12 Step Prayers for A Way Out*, page 40)

Step Four laid the foundation for identifying many of our shadowy deeds and thoughts. It also provided an opportunity for recording our strengths. Completing our Step Four inventory made us aware of many truths about ourselves. This realization may have caused us pain. The natural reaction is to feel sadness or guilt or both. We faced ourselves and our history honestly. We courageously identified some behaviors we want to eliminate.

For those of us who have been honest and thorough, Step Four has provided the foundation upon which we will build our recovery. It identified the unresolved feelings, unhealed memories, and personal defects that produced resentment, depression, and loss of self-worth. Our Higher Power helped us commit our lives to walking in the light of truth. The acknowledgment of our wrongs and the mending of our self-worth have begun to lift a great burden from our hearts and minds. Now that we have identified our character traits, it is possible to relieve ourselves of the burden of guilt and shame associated with our wrongdoings.

Step Five requires that we engage in honest confrontations with ourselves and others by admitting our faults to God, to ourselves, and to another person. By doing so, we begin the important phase of setting aside our pride so that we can see ourselves in true perspective.

Admitting the exact nature of our wrongs to God is the first phase of Step Five. Here, we admit to God all that we have worked so hard to conceal. It is no longer necessary to blame God or others for what has happened to us. We begin to accept our history for exactly what it is. This process of acceptance brings us closer to our Higher Power, and we start to realize that our Higher Power is always there for us.

Admitting our wrongs to ourselves began in Step Four, as we wrote our inventory and had the opportunity to see our behaviors for what they really are. In Step Five, we consciously admit our wrongs. This increases our self-esteem and supports us as we move toward Step Seven, in which we ask God to remove our shortcomings.

Telling our story to another person can be a frightening experience. Many of us have spent a major portion of our lives building defenses to keep others out. Living in isolation has been a way of protecting ourselves from further hurt. Step Five is our pathway out of isolation and loneliness, a move toward wholeness, happiness, and a sense of peace. It is a humbling experience to be totally honest, but we can no longer pretend. It is time to reveal ourselves completely.

We will unveil parts of our nature that we have concealed from ourselves. We may fear the impact that telling the truth will have on our lives. sharing our story with another person may cause us additional fear of being rejected. However, it is essential that we take this important risk and admit our wrongs. With our Higher Power's help, we will have the courage to reveal our true nature. The result will be worth all the agony of the unburdening process.

Following are some important guidelines to focus on when completing the fifth step. Begin with resentment and fear in Step Four, then proceed by reviewing the other traits you wrote about.

- Remember that Step Five asks only that we admit the exact nature of our wrongs. We admit how our behaviors have been hurtful to ourselves and others. It is not necessary to discuss how the wrongs came about or how changes will be made. You are not seeking counsel or advice.

- Remember also to share your strengths. The objective is balance. Thank God for the strengths of character that are a part of your life.

- Begin with prayer, calling upon your Higher Power to be present as you prepare to go through your fourth step revelations and insights. Ask God to guide and support you in what you are about to experience.

- After completing your fifth step, take time for prayer and meditation to reflect on what you have done. Thank your Higher Power for the tools you have been given to improve your relationship with him. Spend time rereading the first five steps and note anything you have omitted. Acknowledge that you are laying a new foundation for your life. The cornerstone is your relationship with God and your commitment to honesty and humility.

- Congratulate yourself for having the courage to risk self-disclosure, and thank God for the peace of mind you have achieved.

Ask for God's help in choosing the person to whom you will admit your wrongs. God intended us to speak to others, to share our sorrows and joys. Look for qualities you admire in the other person that will inspire your confidence.

Choose your Fifth Step listener carefully, one who is familiar with Twelve-Step programs. The individual can be:

- A member of a Twelve-Step program. If you are working with family groups, you may find that significant trust already exists in your group. That trust will deepen by doing your fifth step with a group member.

- A clergyman ordained by an established religion. Ministers of many faiths often receive such requests.

- A trusted friend (preferably of the same sex), a doctor, or psychologist.

- A family member with whom you can openly share. Be careful not to reveal information that might be harmful to your spouse or other family members.

- Choose a listener who is patient and sympathetic. The listener is God's spokesperson and is communicating God's unconditional acceptance.

- Choose a listener who is accepting and understanding.

PERSONAL REFLECTION

Our growing relationship with our Higher Power gave us the courage to examine ourselves, accept who we are, and reveal our true selves. Step Five helps us acknowledge and discard our old survival skills and move toward a new and healthier life. Being thorough and honest in completing our inventory places us in a position to move forward. We will share all we have learned about ourselves.

Step Five consists of three distinct parts. We will admit our faults to God, to ourselves, and to another human being. For some of us, it will involve telling our life story for the first time. As we do it, we will cleanse ourselves of the excess baggage we have been carrying. As we open our hearts and reveal ourselves, we will achieve a deeper level of spirituality.

We begin Step Five by admitting our wrongs to God. This brings us closer to ultimately surrendering to a Higher Power—"Letting Go and Letting God." To attain this goal, we must give up our need to control things and offer ourselves, our desired outcomes and our lives to our compassionate Higher Power. Admitting our wrongs to God is not for God's benefit. It is an opportunity for us to know that our Higher Power loves us and is patiently waiting for us to admit to and learn from our ineffective behavior.

In doing this we experience an inner acceptance of our Higher Power and others.

The following information is helpful when completing your fifth step with God:

- Imagine your Higher Power sitting across from you in a chair.

- Start with a prayer such as, "Higher Power, I understand that you already know me completely. I am now ready to reveal myself to you openly and humbly—my hurtful behaviors, self-centeredness, and negative traits. I am grateful to you for the gifts and abilities that have brought me to this point in my life. Take away my fear of being known and rejected. I place myself and my life in your care and keeping."

- Speak audibly, sincerely, and honestly. Share your understanding of the insights you gained from your fourth step inventory. Be aware that emotions may surface as part of the powerful cleansing experience taking place.

IF YOU HAVE NOT ALREADY DONE IT, STOP NOW AND COMPLETE YOUR FIFTH STEP WITH GOD.

Our admission to ourselves is the least-threatening part of Step Five and it can be done with the least risk. However, it is not the easiest part of Step Five because of denial. We use denial as a coping mechanism—an unconscious tool to protect ourselves from pain. Through denial we are protected from facing the truth about ourselves. Denial is not easily conquered, but if we have done an honest Step Four inventory, the barrier of denial is already weakened.

The following information is helpful when completing your fifth step with yourself:

- Writing your fourth step inventory began the process of developing your self-awareness, the first step toward what will become genuine self-love. Solitary self-appraisal is the beginning of your admission, but it is not enough by itself. It is in Step Five is that you turn that knowledge into improved self-acceptance.

- Sit in a chair with your imaginary double seated across from you in an empty chair. Or sit in front of a mirror that allows you to see yourself as you speak.

- Speak out loud. Allow yourself time to hear what you are saying and to note any deeper understanding that occurs.

- Acknowledge your courage for proceeding to this point. This and every part of this process releases excess emotional baggage that you have carried around because of low self-worth.

IF YOU HAVE NOT ALREADY DONE IT,
STOP NOW AND COMPLETE YOUR FIFTH STEP
INVENTORY WITH YOURSELF.

Admitting our wrongs to another human being is the most powerful part of Step Five. It is a true exercise in humility and will help us break down our defenses. Being rigorously honest with another human being may frighten us and cause us to procrastinate this portion of Step Five. Admitting our wrongs to another person provides us with special healing and wholeness and releases the grip that our hidden secrets have on us.

When choosing a person for Step Five, we will want to select a loving, caring person, one who will be there for us and who will provide unconditional acceptance. The person must be dependable, trustworthy, and not shocked or offended by what we reveal. It is wise to choose someone who is familiar with the program. Sharing will flow easily if there is honesty and opportunities for feedback from the other person. Trusting the person with whom we share our story is vital to the success of Step Five and will provide a safe atmosphere.

In telling our story to another person, we can expect more than just being heard. We must be ready to listen to the other person's response. The interchange can be helpful and productive if we are willing to listen with an open mind to the other person's viewpoint. This broadens our awareness of ourselves and gives us an opportunity to change and grow. Feedback is vital to us as a means of completing the process of revelation. Questions asked in a caring and understanding manner can reveal new insights and feelings. Sharing our life story in this way can be one of the most important interactions in our lives.

It takes considerable humility to bare ourselves to another person. We are about to reveal our self-defeating, damaging, and harmful character traits. We also will mention our positive strengths and worthwhile traits. We must do this to remove the masks we present to the world. It is a bold step toward eliminating our need for pretense and hiding. Rigorous honesty should be our goal, not personal image. We all want the respect and admiration of others, but the need to be well-thought-of must not interfere with our need for honesty.

The following information is helpful when completing your fifth step with another person:

- Allow ample time to complete each thought and stay focused on the subject. Refrain from unnecessary explanations.

- Eliminate distractions. Telephone calls, children, visitors, and extraneous noises must not disrupt your sharing.

- When Step Five is completed, both parties can share their feelings about the experience. It is now possible to extend to each other the love God extends to us.
- It is possible that you will not see your fifth step listener again. That's OK. It is your decision to continue the relationship in whatever direction you choose, from casual friendship to deeper spiritual companionship.

IF YOU HAVE NOT ALREADY DONE IT,
STOP NOW AND COMPLETE YOUR FIFTH STEP
WITH ANOTHER HUMAN BEING.

When Step Five is completed, some expectations may remain unfulfilled. Our Higher Power's timing is not always our timing. God works in each one of us according to our own capacity to respond. We are not to submit to our anxiety; instead, we are to trust our Higher Power. The real test of our Step Five admission is our willingness to trust that God will strengthen and develop our capacity to change our lives.

Upon completion of Step Five, we will realize that we are not always in control. It is not easy to change our old behavior patterns all at once. Admitting the exact nature of our wrongs is no guarantee we will stop acting in our old ways. We can expect to have moments of weakness. But we can also be strong in knowing that our relationship with God can help us overcome them. If we sincerely want to change our ways, our Higher Power will give us the strength and courage required.

KEY IDEAS

Shadow: In Step Five we come to grips with our shadow. In Step Four we noted the presence of our shadow, but we really didn't confront how it impacted our life. It's like coming to believe that a mouse is at work in our kitchen during the night. In the mornings, we find droppings and teeth marks, but we don't see the mouse itself. In Step Four we noted the evidence and identified the problems, but in Step Five we catch the mouse. We admit to our wrongs openly.

Admission: In Step Five, admission is the act of admitting our wrongs, and acknowledge openly what we have discovered about ourselves in our Step Four inventory. We speak the truth about ourselves; we tell our story. We end the silence, the isolation, the hiding.

STEP SIX

Were entirely ready to have God remove all these defects of character.

Understanding Step Six

When a farmer works a field, he begins by preparing the soil. The farmer will plow, disc, harrow, fertilize, harrow again, and finally plant the seeds. For a period of time the farmer is visibly active in his field. But after he plants, he stops for a while to allow the new seeds to grow. There is nothing he can do except wait and hope for the best.

In Step Six, activity ceases for a season. The seeds of change that our Higher Power planted are allowed time to germinate and grow. Our emotions are allowed time to catch up with our new experiences. We have been plowed and prepared, and now we give God's power the necessary time to create in us an internal change. This internal change is a growing readiness and willingness to have God remove all of our defects of character. We might, on the surface, think that this is an easy thing, but many of these defects are deep character traits on which we have depended for survival. To release them means letting go of more than just a defect; it means letting go of a way of life.

Working Step Six

We work Step Six by being ready to have our Higher Power bring change into our lives. Becoming ready may not seem a lot like work, but it is—it's spiritual work. God can't change us unless we are willing to allow it, and so far we have not asked God for change. We have only become aware of our condition and admitted our need. In future steps we will ask our Higher Power to remove our shortcomings and to help us set things straight. In this step we wait for God to do some internal work, and we must be sensitive to the changes being made in our hearts.

Preparing for Step Six

We prepare for Step Six by quieting our minds and opening our hearts. Steps Four and Five required a lot of hard work and brought up some painful discoveries about ourselves. Now we can best prepare for the next leg of the journey by making quiet time for ourselves. We put down the pencils and put on the walking shoes. Taking time to be alone with ourselves and with our Higher Power helps us to remove the distractions that sometimes shield us from reality.

Prayer for Step Six

Quiet My Heart

Quiet my heart, God,
From all the activity and noise.
Help me center my thoughts, my mind.
Remove the distractions that spin me.
My wrongs, my faults lie before you.
You know me inside out, the good and the bad.
Help me receive your inner working and change.
I want to turn my back on yesterday's ways.
I want to truly desire change, lasting change.
So quiet my heart, make me ready.

(Taken from *12 Step Prayers for A Way Out,* page 47)

Having completed Steps One through Five, some of us may believe that we can stop here. The truth is much more work lies ahead. The best results are yet to come. In Steps One and Two, we recognized our powerlessness and came to believe in a power greater than ourselves. In Step Three, we turned our wills and our lives over to God's care. In Steps Four and Five we honestly faced the truth about ourselves and admitted that truth to God, to ourselves, and to another person. We may have an illusion that everything is OK and that the remaining steps are less important. If we believe this, we will surely undermine our progress.

Steps One through Five helped to steer us in the right direction as we built a foundation for ultimate surrender. In Step Six, we confront the need to change our attitudes and behaviors. Here, we prepare to make these changes and totally alter the course of our lives.

The changes that are about to take place in our lives require a cooperative effort. Our Higher Power provides the direction and plants the desire. We contribute the willingness to take the action required. Our job is to respond to Our Higher Power's leadership in our journey. God never forces himself on us; we must invite God into our lives. That is why Step Six is so important. This step provides us with the opportunity to become ready for God's deepest work, which is yet to come.

We are not expected to remove our character defects alone. We are expected only to be entirely ready to "Let go and let God." Step Six is not an action step. It is a state of preparation that helps us to become ready to release our faults to God. Our willingness to surrender will increase. This enables us to reach the point (in Step Seven) where we ask God to take over and remove our faults. We do this by working the program, one day at a time, regardless of whether or not we see any progress.

We must remind ourselves that the character traits we want to eliminate are often deeply ingrained patterns of behavior, developed through many years of struggling to survive. They will not vanish overnight. We must be patient while God is reshaping us. Through our new willingness to let our Higher Power be in control, we learn to trust more completely and welcome our Higher Power's timetable for our growth.

Step Six is similar to Step Two. Both steps deal with our willingness to allow God to work through us to change our lives. In Step Two, we seek restoration to sanity by coming to believe in a power greater than ourselves. In Step Six, we seek readiness to let God remove our short-comings. Both steps acknowledge the existence of problems and require that we seek our Higher Power's help in being freed from them. The fact that we "came to believe" will strengthen our capacity to be "entirely ready."

PERSONAL REFLECTION

To be successful with Step Six, we must sincerely want to change our disabling behaviors. But even this desire to change will come from our Higher Power's guidance as we wait upon God's will for our lives. Our past has been dominated by our self-will. We victimized ourselves by our self-will, rarely calling on God for help. Our life's condition shows us that self-will has never been enough to help us. Now, honest determination to eliminate our behavior flaws causes us to seek God's will. Before we can accept our Higher Power's help, we must relinquish our self-destructive natures.

At this point in our program, we see that change is nec-essary to live life to the fullest. Recognizing the need for change and being willing to change are two different matters. The space between recognition and willingness to change can be filled with fear. As we move toward willingness, we must let go of our fears and remain secure in the knowledge that with God's guidance, everything will be restored to us. We let go of fear by holding on to God's love. When we firmly hold on to the fact that our Higher Power loves us, we will find it easier to change.

Our character defects are familiar tools to us. They are what we used as coping mechanisms to deal with our surroundings. The loss of these tools threatens our ability to control ourselves and others. The thought of giving up our character defects may cause anxiety. But we can trust that God won't remove a character trait we need. When we place our trust in God we develop a sense of comfort. Even the smallest beginning is acceptable to our Higher Power. One sure way to hinder our growth is to think we are able to make the necessary changes ourselves. Healing requires God, not self-will.

Our ability to talk to our Higher Power is an important part of Step Six. We need to communicate in a way that shows our humility and invites intervention. When we say, "Dear God, I want to be more patient," we are making a demand and telling God what we want. When we say "Dear God, I am impatient," we present the truth about ourselves. When we pray in this manner, we exhibit humility, relinquish our pride, and ask God to act on our behalf.

This step requires that we look at the shortcomings we will ask to have removed. We may be unwilling to give up some of them. They may seem useful to us, so we respond, "I cannot give up...yet." We have a potential problem if we say "I will never be any different and will never give up." These attitudes shut our minds to God's redeeming qualities and can add to our own destruction. If we respond this way to any behavior, we need to admit our doubts and struggles to our Higher Power and seek help in surrendering to our will.

"BROKEN DREAMS"

As children bring their broken toys
with tears for us to mend,
I brought my broken dreams to God
because He was my friend.
But then, instead of leaving Him
in peace to work alone,
I hung around and tried to help
with ways that were my own.
At last, I snatched them back and cried,
"How can you be so slow?"
"My child," He said,
"What could I do?
"You never did let go."

Author unknown

As we follow the principles of the program in our daily lives, we gradually and unconsciously prepare to have our shortcomings removed. Sometimes, we are even unaware of our readiness to have our defects removed. At first, we realize that we are behaving differently—that we have changed. Sometimes, others note the changes before we become aware of them ourselves. Approval seekers begin to function more independently; control addicts become more easygoing and more relaxed; caretakers become more sensitive to their own needs. People who diligently work the program as an integral part of their lives become calmer, more serene, and genuinely happy.

A radiant, confident person lives in each of us, hidden under a cloud of confusion and uncertainty, distracted by ineffective behavior. If someone asked us if we wanted to be freed from our character defects, we could give only one answer—we are entirely ready to have God remove them from us.

KEY IDEAS

Readiness: Step Six is a time to overcome fear and gather the readiness we need to proceed with our recovery. We now know the truth about ourselves and what faults must be removed. In Step Six we need readiness and willingness to allow God to change us. This step is like bungee jumping. You may be dressed to jump, and have all the facts about the bungee cord. You may even have complete confidence in the operators, but you won't jump until you're ready. And you won't be ready until you overcome your fear. Your defects are a part of you. They have helped you survive. The thought of losing anything, even your damaging defects, tends to produce fear.

Defects of Character: Our defects of character are called many things in the program. They are called character weaknesses, faults, shortcomings, harmful behaviors, survival skills, negative traits, etc. Whatever the name, the point is the same. These undesirable parts of ourselves must be removed and replaced with godly character. These defects of character began innocently in childhood. They were our means of survival. We learned to manipulate in order to have our needs met, to lie to protect ourselves, and to hide our emotions in defense against overwhelming pain. In short, we learned how to survive. These survival skills were tools of control. They were our ways of managing our environment, minimizing our threats, and taking care of ourselves. Eventually, these coping skills break down. It is then we realize that God is the only one able and wise enough to control our lives.

Willingness: Willingness is a state of mind and emotions that propels us into action. We may have the best intentions, but until we are willing to act, we won't. There are many singles today who want to get married, who intend to get married, and who even know whom to marry, but they won't marry because they are not yet willing. In Step Six all of our good intentions simmer and brew until, with God's help, we are entirely ready and willing to change.

STEP SEVEN

Humbly asked God to remove our shortcomings.

Understanding Step Seven

Anyone who has been seriously ill or injured knows what it's like to need others. It is indeed humbling when we are in that sickbed and unable to move or care for ourselves. Even the simplest of needs must be met by another. By the time we come to Step Seven we realize that we are on a sickbed, and the only one who can meet our needs is God. Every step, up till now, has reinforced the same theme: We are unable, but God is able.

By Step Seven we have abandoned the illusion that we can help ourselves. The pain of our former way of life has caught up to us, and we lie wounded with a self-inflicted injury. We are certainly not interested in doing it by ourselves now. So as we lie helpless and humbled on the sickbed of our disease, we pray: "Remove my shortcomings."

Working Step Seven

Step Seven requires prayer. We work this step on our knees. Our condition, our honesty, and our pain have humbled us so now we must open our mouths and pray. The temptation here is to pray a general prayer. We are tempted to ask God to remove everything as if it were a package deal. But that's not how the program works. If we were thorough, our Step Four inventory listed each character defect separately. Our admission in Step Five was also done item by item, and later our amends will be made individually. So now our Step Seven work is humble prayer for the removal of our shortcomings—one defect at a time.

Preparing for Step Seven

We prepare for Step Seven by holding nothing back from our Higher Power—no glimmer of hope in our own ability to control. We prepare for Step Seven by making sure that we have resolved the fear of letting go of our defects. We prepare for Step Seven by learning to draw nearer to God, by becoming comfortable in God's presence. We prepare by taking prayer seriously. This is a time to talk to our Higher Power in a very personal way about our Step Four inventory

Prayer for Step Seven

Prayer for Healing

Higher Power,

You have told us to ask and we will receive, to seek and we will find, to knock and you will open the door to us.

I trust in your love for me and in the healing power of your compassion. I praise you and thank you for the mercy you have shown to me.

Higher Power, I am sorry for all my mistakes. I ask for your help in removing the negative patterns of my life. I accept with all my heart your forgiving love.

And I ask for the grace to be aware of the character defects that exist within myself. Let me not offend you by my weak human nature or by my impatience, resentment, or neglect of people who are a part of my life. Rather, teach me the gift of understanding and the ability to forgive, just as you continue to forgive me.

I seek your strength and your peace so that I may become your instrument in sharing those gifts with others.

Guide me in my prayer that I might know what needs to be healed and how to ask you for that healing.

It is you, Higher Power, whom I seek. Please enter the door of my heart and fill me with the presence of your spirit now and forever.

I thank you, God, for doing this.

(Taken from *12 Step Prayers for A Way Out*, page 53-54)

Humility is a recurring theme in the Twelve-Step program and the central idea of Step Seven. By practicing humility we receive the tools necessary to work the program and achieve satisfactory results. We recognize now, more than ever before, that most of our lives have been devoted to fulfilling our self-centered desires. We must set aside these prideful, less-than-nurturing behaviors, come to terms with our inadequacies, and realize that humbly seeking God's will alone will free our spirit. Step Seven requires surrendering our will to God so that we may receive the serenity necessary to achieve the happiness we seek.

We are growing in the wisdom and knowledge of our Higher Power. This growth not only comes because we are seeking it, but also from the insight gained by examining the pain of our past struggles. We gain greater courage by hearing how others cope with their life challenges. As we work through the steps, we recognize the value of acknowledging the truth of our past. Although the pain of this reality may seem unbearable, the insights we achieve are the only means to our release.

Step Six prepared us to let go of our old defective behaviors and freed us to develop the powerful new ones that God intends for us to use. Asking God to remove our faults is a true measure of our willingness to surrender

THE TWELVE STEPS FOR ADULT CHILDREN

control. For many of us, the surrender of control can be an extremely difficult task—but not impossible. Are we sincerely ready to abandon these deceptions? If so, then we can ask God to help us let go of our past and create new life within us.

Step Seven is a vitally important part of the cleansing process and prepares us for the next stage of our journey. During the first six steps, we became aware of our problems, looked at our lives honestly, revealed previously hidden aspects of ourselves, and became ready to change our attitudes and behaviors. Step Seven presents us with the opportunity to turn to our Higher Power and ask for removal of those parts of our character that cause us pain.

Before beginning this program, we avoided looking at ourselves honestly and admitting the extent of our disabling behavior. Meditating on the vision of God's presence in our lives will focus our attention on living life according to our Higher Power's example and begin to free us from this disabling burden of "self." Our partnership with our Higher Power will put our obsession with "self" into its proper perspective. We will finally recognize the person we have been, understand who we are, and look forward with joy to the person we are becoming.

Preparing to have our shortcomings removed requires willingness to work with God to revise and redirect our attention and activity. Our progress will be halted if we continue our destructive behaviors. We must be ever-vigilant and alert to the possible return of "old behaviors" and work diligently toward eliminating them from our lives. It is wise to be gentle with ourselves and remember that it took us a lifetime to develop these habits. It is not realistic to expect them to disappear overnight.

When looking to God to remove our shortcomings, we do well to remember that God gives strength to us through prayer and meditation and also through other people. God often uses outside forces to correct our defects. Teachers, ministers, medical doctors, and therapists can all be instruments of our Higher Power's work. Our willingness to seek outside help can be a clear indication of our readiness to change. Compulsive worriers can pray to God to release their worries and, at the same time, seek help from a counselor to relieve their anxiety. Persons who overindulge in food or drugs can seek professional help to gain control over their obsessive habits. We need to pray for God's help in removing our shortcomings, and have the courage to seek professional help when we know we need it.

PERSONAL REFLECTION

Through working the steps, we are progressing toward a happier and healthier life. We see how the opportunities and blessings that God brings into our lives surpass anything we could ever have created on our own. Having completed the first six steps, we are becoming aware of the multitude of benefits available to us. Through this awareness, we become grateful for God's presence and secure in the knowledge that our lives are improving.

Step Seven implies that we ask for removal of all our shortcomings. However, the process will be more manageable if we deal with them individually, working on the easiest ones first to build up our confidence and strength. If we are patient, God will see that we achieve our goal at a pace that is comfortable for us. Our willingness to accept God's help builds trust and confidence in ourselves and in our Higher Power. For now, use your Step Four inventory as your Step Seven guide to prayer. Remember that faith is required when you humbly ask God to remove your shortcomings. Trust that God hears and desires to answer, regardless of your emotions. You may not feel or experience any immediate change after you pray. Be confident, however, that your Higher Power has heard your request and will work to remove your shortcomings.

We may find that after we ask God to relieve us of a burdensome behavior, it doesn't seem to go away. Becoming angry or discouraged is understandable but self-defeating. It is more productive to reach out and ask for prayer support from a friend in recovery. It helps to express our negative feelings to our Higher Power in prayer, knowing that God understands. When things do not seem to go according to our timetable, reciting the Serenity Prayer can also work to our advantage. It reminds us that God can give us serenity to accept the things we cannot change.

"PARADOXES OF PRAYER"

I asked God for strength, that I might achieve
I was made weak, that I might learn humbly to obey...
I asked for health, that I might do greater things
I was given infirmity, that I might do better things...
I asked for riches, that I might be happy
I was given poverty, that I might be wise...
I asked for power,
that I might have the praise of men
I was given weakness,
that I might feel the need of God...
I asked for all things, that I might enjoy life
I was given life, that I might enjoy all things...
I got nothing that I asked for—
but everything I had hoped for
Almost despite myself,
my unspoken prayers were answered
I am, among all, most richly blessed!
© Universal Press Syndicate

Letting go of negative behaviors, however destructive they are, may create a sense of loss and require that we allow ourselves time to grieve. Some of our negative character traits are like old friends. They may be inappropriate and even hurtful to us, but we still mourn losing them. It is normal to grieve for the loss of something we no longer have. In our childhood we may have experienced "things" being taken from us abruptly or before we were ready to release them. Now, we may be too sensitive and cling to "things" to avoid the pain of loss. So that we don't avoid or deny the existence of our fear of letting go, we can turn to our Higher Power for courage and trust the outcome to him. This is an opportunity to rely on our love and trust in God to heal our memories, repair the damage, and restore us to wholeness.

Changing our behavior can be temporarily alarming to our sense of self. Our fear of not knowing what is ahead may cause us to repeat past destructive actions. We may retreat into feeling isolated and lose our sense of belonging. Having faith and trusting in our relationship with our Higher Power shows our willingness to release the fear of being lost, frightened, or abandoned. Our Higher Power wants to be our new escape, the one to whom we run when we experience pain or discomfort.

As we notice our defects being removed and our lives becoming less complicated, we must proceed with caution and guard against the temptation to be prideful. Sudden changes in our behavior can and do happen, but we cannot anticipate them or direct them. God initiates change when we are ready, and we cannot claim that we alone removed our character defects. When we learn to ask humbly for God's help in our lives, change becomes God's responsibility. We cannot accept the credit, but we can give thanks. When good changes begin to happen in our lives, we tend to expect similar changes in others. But our focus needs to remain on ourselves—we still have much to accomplish.

Destructive behaviors that remain after we complete Step Seven may never be eliminated. However, we have an opportunity to transform these aspects of our character into positive traits and learn to use them in a constructive way. Leaders may be left with a quest for power but with no need to misuse it. Lovers will be left with exceptional sensuality but with enough sensitivity to refrain from causing pain to the person they love. Those who are materially wealthy may continue to have plenty, but will set aside their greed and possessiveness. With the help of our Higher Power, all aspects of our personal lives can be rewarding and fulfilling. By continuing to practice humility and accept the tools God is giving us, we will eventually begin to aspire to a more peaceful life, sharing with others the love we have received.

For the program to be successful, we must practice the steps regularly. When we have moments of inner struggle, we can simply say, "This too will pass"; "I let go and let God"; "I fear no evil"; "I choose to see the good in this experience." These affirmations are useful to keep us from reverting to our obsessive/compulsive behaviors. Depression, guilt, and anger can be acknowledged and understood to be temporary reactions.

We need to stop for a moment and acknowledge ourselves for our commitment to recovery. Note how determination enabled us to break the bonds of our unhealthy habits and behaviors. We can accept the positive, spontaneous thoughts and feelings that occur and see that this acceptance results from our personal relationship with God. We learn that the guidance we receive from our Higher Power is always available. All we need to do is listen and act without fear.

KEY IDEAS

Humility: Many of us in recovery misunderstand humility. If we are co-dependent, we might mistakenly think that humility is doing for others and placing ourselves second. True humility is seeing ourselves as we really are. By Step Seven, we have a new and, hopefully, honest understanding of ourselves. We also have an honest understanding of our need for a Higher Power. Seeing our character defects and shortcomings has made us realize that we cannot change ourselves without divine help. When we honestly realize our shortcomings, our needs, and our powerlessness to change ourselves, we can't help but come to our Higher Power in humility.

Shortcomings: Shortcomings are our unwelcome behaviors, character defects, survival skills, self-defeating attitudes, harmful resentments, destructive fears, etc. that have been revealed to us in the process of working the program. Although other descriptive words have been used, we have been focusing on our shortcomings for three steps now. In Step Four we listed them; in Step Five we admitted them to God, to ourselves, and to another human being. In Step Six we became entirely ready to have God remove these defects of character. Now, in Step Seven we humbly ask God to remove our shortcomings.

STEP EIGHT

Made a list of all persons we had harmed, and became willing to make amends to them all.

Understanding Step Eight

"Mom! Sarah hit me!" R. J. screamed like a siren.

"But he kicked me first," Sarah answered in defense.

"Yeah, but she took my game."

"He shouldn't be so touchy."

And so it goes. Does this sound familiar? Kids love to blame others for their troubles, and they hate to accept any responsibility. We adults might occasionally compel them to accept responsibility and coerce them into a forced apology. But they would never freely choose to say, "I'm sorry. My behavior was out of line."

In Step Eight we begin to grow up. We take responsibility for our actions without consideration for the wrongs done to us by others. In the first seven steps we have dealt with our own stuff. Step Four was *our* moral inventory—it was for our benefit, nobody else's. Our Step Five admissions were for *our* wrongs. The shortcomings belong to us. In Step Eight, we continue to look at ourselves. But this time, we are considering those people who were harmed by our character defects.

Working Step Eight

We work Step Eight with thoughtful reflection. With God's help, we recall the names and faces of people we have harmed. Our job is to write their names down and consider each person carefully. We need to examine our relationship with these people and consider how we have harmed them. We will help ourselves by being as thorough as possible in our considerations and notes.

Preparing for Step Eight

We prepare for Step Eight through practicing humility. The willingness to be humble puts our lives in proper perspective and places us in agreement with God's plan and will for our lives. Step Eight requires that we recognize our part in the harm that has been done to others and not focus on the harm that has been done to us.

On a practical note, we prepare for Step Eight by taking time for reflection. This may mean attending a retreat or setting aside time to be quiet and thoughtful.

Prayer for Step Eight

It's About Me

Help me remember, God, that this program is about me. I find myself wanting to judge and blame and accuse everyone but myself. I'm supposed to be making a list of all those I have harmed, yet my mind is full of those who have offended me. Is this some sort of mental defense mechanism to keep myself from facing the pain I've caused others?

Help me get over this stumbling block. I release those who hurt me. I forgive. I put those people in your hands, God. Vengeance is yours. Wait God...don't punish them. I'm just as guilty...don't punish me.

Help me make things right.

(Taken from *12 Step Prayers for A Way Out,* page 61)

Before entering the Twelve-Step program, many of us blamed our parents, relatives, and friends for the turmoil in our lives. We even held God responsible. In Step Eight, we begin the process of releasing the need to blame others for our misfortune and accepting full responsibility for our own lives. Our fourth step inventory revealed that our inappropriate behavior caused injury not only to us but also to the significant others in our lives. Now we must prepare to accept full responsibility and make amends.

Steps One through Seven helped us to center ourselves in the healing power of the Twelve Steps. We were given the tools to examine our personal experiences and to see the importance of letting go of the past. We were freed to continue our personal growth by facing our history and putting it behind us. Like barnacles on a ship's hull, our past wrongdoings can prevent us from sailing smoothly to a life filled with peace.

Working Steps Eight and Nine will improve our relationships, both with ourselves and others. These steps also invite us to leave behind our isolation and loneliness. The key factor here is our willingness to make amends to those we have harmed. As we continue to welcome our Higher Power's presence into our hearts, we will develop a new openness with others. This openness will prepare us for the face-to-face amends to follow. In Step Eight, we examine each past misdeed and identify the persons involved. Our intention is to make amends and heal our past so that God can transform the present.

Reviewing our fourth step inventory will help us determine who belongs on our list. Making amends is a difficult task— one that we will execute with increasing skill, yet never really finish. Again, uncomfortable feelings may surface as we come to grips with our past behaviors. As we recognize the damage caused by our actions, we will realize what great relief awaits us when we no longer cause injury to ourselves and others.

For many of us, admitting our misdeeds and making the necessary amends will be difficult. The pattern of our lives has been to blame others and to seek retribution for the wrongs done to us. When we look at ourselves, we see that the retribution we vainly sought only created more havoc. By insisting on our own measure of justice, we lost the ability to set and achieve positive goals. Cycles of hatred and hard feelings were created, and we kept our attention focused away from our own wrongs.

Forgiving ourselves and others helps us overcome our resentments. Our Higher Power has already forgiven us for the harmful actions that alienated us from God. Developing the ability to forgive ourselves is an important element in our ongoing recovery. The ability to forgive others is essential. Amends without forgiveness lead to dishonesty and further complicate our lives.

To repair our past wrongdoings, we must be willing to face those wrongs by recording the harm we think we have caused. When preparing the list of people we have harmed, it is best to keep our thoughts directed toward making things right. Although our intentions may be rebuffed, our desire is to obey God and find healing. People on our list may feel bitter toward us and resist our attempts at restitution. They may hold deep grudges and be unwilling to reconcile with us. No matter how we are received, we must be willing to proceed with our amends. The amends we make are principally for our own benefit, not the benefit of those we have harmed.

The following are three main categories in which we may have caused harm and for which we must be willing to make amends.

Material Wrongs: Actions that affected an individual in a tangible way, including: borrowing or spending extravagance; stinginess; spending in an attempt to buy friendship or love; withholding money in order to gratify yourself. Entering agreements that are legally enforceable, then refusing to abide by the terms or simply cheating. Injuring or damaging persons or property because of our actions.

Moral Wrongs: Inappropriate behavior in moral or ethical actions and conduct, including questions of rightness, fairness, or equity. The principal issue is involving others in our wrongdoing: setting a bad example for children, friends, or anyone who looks to us for guidance. Being preoccupied with selfish pursuits and totally unaware of the needs of others. Forgetting birthdays, holidays, and other special occasions. Inflicting moral harm (e.g., sexual infidelity, broken promises, verbal abuse, lack of trust, lying).

Spiritual Wrongs: "Acts of omission" by neglecting our obligations to God, to ourselves, to family, and to community. Making no effort to fulfill our obligations and showing no gratitude toward others who have helped us. Avoiding self-development (e.g., health, education, recreation, creativity). Being inattentive to others in our lives by showing a lack of encouragement to them.

PERSONAL REFLECTION

Step Eight begins the process of healing damaged relationships through our willingness to make amends for past misdeeds. We can let go of our resentments and start to overcome the guilt, shame, and low self-esteem we have found through our harmful actions. We can leave behind the gray, angry world of loneliness and move toward a bright future by exercising our new willingness to make things right. Through the gifts of God's work and the Twelve Steps, we have the necessary tools to overcome past wreckage and mend our broken relationships.

To find fulfillment in recovery, we first learn to identify our feelings of guilt, shame, resentment, and low self-worth. Once we identify these feelings, we then ask our Higher Power for help in removing them. This may seem like an awesome task, because we probably have been controlled by these negative feelings for as long as we can remember. Now, for the first time, we have an opportunity to experience a sense of personal integrity and self-authority by working the Steps. We can put our faith and trust in this process, because it has worked miracles for millions of people.

The first part of Step Eight specifically states that we list those persons whom we have harmed. When making the list, many of us may encounter a wall of resistance. It can be a severe shock to realize that we must make face-to-face admissions of our past wrongs to those with whom we have had conflict. It was humiliating enough to admit our wrongs to God, to ourselves, and to another human being in Step Five. In Step Nine, we will actually make direct contact with the people concerned.

We start Step Eight by making a list of the people with whom we feel uncomfortable. We make the list without being concerned about the details; simply making the list enables us to follow where our mind takes us. The list may include family members, business associates, friends, creditors, neighbors. Its length is not important, yet the list may reveal a somewhat unrealistic view of what we believe to be the power of our own personal influence. Step Eight prepares us for the ongoing process of healing that this program offers. Our willingness to risk honesty enables the healing to take place.

Step Eight asks that we face the truth of our behavior and become willing to make amends. We should be prepared to willingly accept the consequences and take whatever measures are necessary to make restitution. This means acknowledging our part in the circumstances where someone was harmed as a result of our behavior. Accepting responsibility and making appropriate restitution are vitally important activities. Only through expressing genuine regret for our behavior can we complete the housecleaning necessary for putting the past behind us and achieving the peace and serenity we desire.

Willingness is a key element in completing Step Eight. Being willing to forgive ourselves and those who have caused us harm is an important aspect of this process. This may require a great deal of humility from us. We are already aware that having resentments and holding grudges are luxuries we cannot afford—they not only destroy our serenity and well being but they are more harmful to us than to the persons we resent. Harboring a resentment or grudge is like having an open wound eating away at us. It causes discomfort and makes us angry, bitter, and ill-tempered. These feelings can deplete our energy, making it difficult for others to be in our presence.

Occasionally we will be prevented from facing the people on our list directly. They may be deceased, separated from us, or unwilling to meet with us. Whatever the situation, we still need to put them on our list. When we make the amends in Step Nine, we will see why amends are necessary, even if they cannot be made face-to-face. Being willing to make the amends will release us from hard feelings and enable us to experience serenity and peace of mind.

When looking at those persons we have harmed, we see how our character defects have played a major part in sabotaging our lives and our relationships. For example:

- When we became angry, we often harmed ourselves more than others. This may have resulted in feelings of depression or self-pity.

- Persistent financial problems resulting from our irresponsible actions caused difficulty with our family and creditors.

- When confronted with an issue about which we felt guilty, we lashed out at others instead of looking honestly at ourselves.

- Frustrated by our lack of control, we behaved aggressively and intimidated those around us.

- Because of our indiscriminate sexual behavior, true intimacy was impossible to achieve or maintain.

- Our fear of abandonment sometimes hurt our relationships, because we did not allow others to be themselves. We created dependency and attempted to control their behavior by trying to maintain the relationship the way we wanted it.

When making a list of people for our amends, we need to remember to focus on ourselves. Many of us were victims of self-inflicted pain because we did not have the skills to take care of ourselves appropriately. We spent time and energy trying to be available for everybody and sacrificed ourselves in the process. We may have been our own worst enemy and experienced excessive self-blame, guilt, and shame. Taking time to look at the harm we have inflicted upon ourselves and being willing to forgive ourselves is essential to our continued growth.

In Step Nine, we seek out the people we have harmed and make amends wherever necessary. For now, all we need to do is list them and describe the harmful behavior. The consequences of our actions may have produced emotional, financial, or physical pain for others. We need to take as much time as necessary to reflect on our list and be as thorough as possible. Being totally honest with ourselves is a major factor in our ability to make restitution for our past destructive actions.

KEY IDEAS

Amends: Within the context of the Twelve-Step program, the idea of amends is broadly defined as "repairing the damage of the past." Amends can be as simple as an apology or as complex as restitution for physical or financial liability.

Forgiveness: Forgiveness is a key part of Step Eight. When we work this step and begin to make a list of the persons we have harmed, we immediately think about how others have harmed us. Perhaps this reaction is a defense mechanism—a way to avoid admitting guilt. It doesn't matter why we feel this way; what matters is that we deal with it. We need to forgive those who have hurt us so we can also be forgiven.

AMENDS LIST

Person	Relationship	My Wrong-doing	Effects on Others	Effects on Me
Joan	wife	angry insults	fear, anger	guilt, shame
John	coworker	sexual advances	distrust, shame	loss of self-respect

Made direct amends to such people wherever possible, except when to do so would injure them or others.

Understanding Step Nine

Natural disasters are always gripping news. Earthquakes, hurricanes, forest or brush fires, and floods capture our attention. For a brief time, they are a major focus of our energy. But rarely do we have an opportunity to see the hard work of rebuilding that takes place after the disaster has past. Lives, homes, businesses, and whole communities are often repaired and revived, but the actual impact on us is not the same as if the tragedy happened to us.

Step Nine is similar to the repairs and rebuilding that take place after a disaster. The difference is that we are part of the entire event. Through the process of making amends, we begin to make restitution and mend the damage of our past. In Step Eight we surveyed the damage and made a plan. Now, in Step Nine we go into action, and make amends for our past behavior.

Working Step Nine

Working Step Nine involves making personal or indirect contact with those we have harmed. We review our Step Eight list person by person. We approach each one we can with gentleness, sensitivity, and understanding. Our Higher Power can help us to know the best way to make contact. Some people will require a face-to-face meeting, while other situations may be handled by simply changing our behavior. In some cases, making a direct amend will not be possible, due to circumstances beyond our control. Whatever the case, God provides us with the wisdom and direction we need.

Preparing for Step Nine

We prepare for Step Nine by making our Step Eight list as complete as possible. We should include ourselves on the list, and be prepared to make a personal amend. There is no need to hurry. The important thing is that we become willing to make the amends. As we pray over every name, God will give us special insight and direction and help us overcome the fear and apprehension that arises.

Prayer for Step Nine

Ninth Step Prayer

Higher Power,

I pray for the right attitude to make my amends, being ever mindful not to harm others in the process. I ask for your guidance in making indirect amends. Most important, I will continue to make amends by staying abstinent, helping others, and growing in spiritual progress.

(Taken from *12 Step Prayers for A Way Out,* pages 66-67)

Step Nine completes the forgiveness process that began in Step Four and fulfills our requirement to reconcile with others. In this step, we clear our garden of the dead leaves—we rake up and discard the old habits that are troublesome to us. We are ready to face our faults, to admit the degree of our wrongs, and to ask for and extend forgiveness. Accepting responsibility for the harm done can be a humbling experience because it forces us to admit the effect we have had on others.

The qualities we need in order to work Step Nine effectively are available from our Higher Power. We receive the judgment and careful sense of timing, courage, and stamina we need to accomplish this task. As we become more courageous, it will be easier and safer to talk honestly about our past behavior and admit to others that we have caused them harm.

Making amends helps release us from many of the resentments of our past. We achieve serenity in our lives by seeking forgiveness from those we have harmed and by making restitution where necessary. Without forgiveness, the resentments will continue to undermine our growth. Making amends releases us from guilt and promotes freedom and health in mind and body.

Some people in our lives feel bitter toward us. Others feel threatened by us and resent our changed behavior. We can pray about these people and ask that our Higher Power's wisdom be made known to us. God gives us the discernment to consider the appropriateness of facing these people directly. If we are to forgive ourselves completely, we must first acknowledge the pain that others have endured because of our actions. We can only pray that God will prepare their hearts to receive our amends.

Some stumbling blocks appear in Step Nine. We may procrastinate by telling ourselves "the time is not yet right." We may delay by finding excuses to avoid facing those we have harmed. We must be honest with ourselves and not procrastinate because of fear. Courage is an important requirement for the successful completion of this step. The very spirit of Step Nine is contained in our decision to make restitution and in our readiness to accept the consequences of our past.

Another delaying tactic is the temptation to let bygones be bygones. We rationalize that our past is behind us, that there is no need to stir up more trouble by bringing up issues from our past. We fantasize that amends for past misdeeds are unnecessary, that all we have to do is change our current behavior. It is true that some of our past behaviors may be laid to rest without direct confrontation. Being supported by others during this leg of our journey enables us to face the people and issues on our amends list. Our improved life filled with peace and serenity is closely connected to our being able to confront the fears and resentments of our past.

PERSONAL REFLECTION

In order to complete Step Nine, we need to review our list from Step Eight and decide on the appropriate method to make each amend. Most situations will require direct contact, although some may be handled by simply changing our behavior. Other amends may need to be done indirectly due to circumstances beyond our control. Whichever alternative we choose, it is important that the process of making amends be done when we are ready, and be as complete as possible.

Step Nine has two distinct parts regarding making amends:

"Made Direct Amends to Such People Wherever Possible"

We make direct amends to people who are readily accessible and who can be approached when we are ready. These people include family members, creditors, coworkers, and others to whom we owe an amend. They can be friends, enemies, or people with whom we do business.

As part of making the amend, we must try to repair to the best of our ability the damage that has been done. The other person's response may be surprising to us, especially if our amend is accepted. We may wonder why we waited so long to resolve the conflict. *There are situations that prevent us from making direct personal contact.* These may involve people who are no longer accessible to us or who are deceased. In these cases, indirect amends can satisfy our need for reconciliation. These amends are accomplished through prayer or by writing a letter, as if we were communicating with the absent person. The important thing is that we make the contact necessary to satisfy our need to make the amend. We also can make amends by performing a kindness for someone else we may not even know, but who is connected in some way to the person we have harmed.

"Except When to Do So Would Injure Them or Others"

Step Nine provides for those people to whom we can make only partial restitution because complete disclosure could cause harm to them or others. These people may include spouses, ex-partners, former business associates, or friends. We must analyze the harm they would suffer if complete disclosure was made. This is especially true in cases of infidelity. In such situations, irreparable damage could occur to all parties if a direct amend were made. Even if the matter must be discussed, we should avoid bringing harm to third parties. Amends for infidelity can be made by concentrating sincere affection and attention on persons to whom we have made loving commitments.

There are situations where amends could result in serious consequences. In cases involving potential loss of employment, imprisonment, or alienation from one's family, we need to weigh the consequences carefully. If we delay our amends merely out of fear for ourselves or others, we will ultimately be the ones to suffer. In these situations, we can seek outside guidance from a counselor, minister, or close friend to decide how to proceed. Otherwise, we will delay our growth, and also experience stagnation in our progress toward building a new and healthier life.

There are amends that require deferred action. It is wise to seek counsel in situations where deferred action is required. It is seldom advisable to abruptly approach an individual who still suffers deeply from the injustices we have done. In situations where our own pain is still deeply imbedded, patience might be the wise choice. Timing is important. Our ultimate goals are personal growth and reconciliation. Recklessness and haste might create further injury.

As we have learned, certain situations require special consideration and timing. It is better to proceed slowly and be complete with the amend, rather than hurry and cause more damage. Here, God can be a great source of aid and comfort. We need to be constantly aware that our Higher Power's presence is with us now and will continue to be with us on our journey. Others may not understand or support our amends process, but God stands ready to help see us through this process.

To help in making the amend, take time to pray and meditate, then prepare a schedule listing the persons to contact, what you will say, how you will say it, and when you will say it. Writing letters and making phone calls are acceptable ways of making amends if face-to-face contact is not possible. Sometimes, meeting in person may not be the most desirable approach. The important thing is to make the amend before it is too late. Successful amends making will improve our relationship with those we have harmed and promote better relationships with others.

When working this step, we need to distinguish between amends and apologies. Apologies are appropriate; however, they are not substitutes for making amends. A person can apologize for being late for work, but until the behavior is corrected, an amend cannot be made. It is important to apologize when necessary, but it is more important to commit to changing the unacceptable behavior.

Occasional emotional and spiritual relapses are to be expected and should be dealt with promptly. If not, they will block our ability to make successful amends. When these relapses occur, we must accept them as signals that we are not working the program effectively. Perhaps we have turned away from God by not praying daily and we need to return to Step Three. We may have eliminated something from our inventory and need to return to Step Four. Or we may be unwilling to relinquish a self-defeating behavior and need to return to Step Six.

Steps Eight and Nine help us repair the past. Through these steps, we take responsibility for our part in causing injury to others and make restitution where necessary. We have a chance to redeem ourselves for past misdeeds by making amends, and we can look forward to a healthy and rewarding future life. We are now able to rebuild our self-esteem, achieve peaceful relations with ourselves and others, and live in harmony with our own personal world and with our Higher Power.

KEY IDEAS

Direct Amends: Direct amends are amends that we make personally to those we have harmed. We schedule appointments or plan to meet personally with them. If physical distance is a problem, we can call them on the phone or write a letter. The amend includes sharing with them that we are in a program that requires us to make amends. We request permission to make our amends to them; then we share our amend without blaming them or others. (See Amends to Others Guidelines below.)

Indirect Amends: Indirect amends are nonpersonal amends that we make to those we have harmed. These include amends to someone who is deceased, whose location is unknown, or who is inaccessible for another reason. We can make indirect amends to these people through letters that are not mailed, through prayer to God, or by doing a kindness to someone else such as a family member of the person we have harmed.

Amends To Self: The one person we have often harmed the most is ourself. The amends process would not be complete without taking time to set things right with ourselves. The best way to accomplish this is to write a letter of amends to ourselves and then read it while sitting in front of a mirror. (See Amends to Self Guidelines on page 116.)

AMENDS TO OTHERS GUIDELINES

This is a summary of ideas and procedures that have been useful in preparing for and making the amends in Step Nine. To align yourself with God's will, ask your Higher Power to give you the correct attitude of heart so that you will be able to do the following.

Attitude

- Love and forgive yourself and the person to whom an amend is to be made.

- Be careful not to blame the person with whom you are communicating.

- Take responsibility for what you are going to say.

- Be willing to accept the consequences.

- Resist the desire for a specific response from the other person.

- Be willing to turn your anxieties over to your Higher Power.

Preparation

- Devote time to prayer and meditation.

- Delay the amend if you are angry or upset.

- Keep it simple. Details and explanations aren't necessary.

- Remember the amend is not about the other person's part in the situation.

- Express your desire or ask permission to make the amend.

Sample Amends

- "I was _____ (scared, overwhelmed, feeling abandoned, etc.) when _____ happened between us. I ask your forgiveness for _____ (harm done) and for anything else I may have done in the past through my thoughts, words, or actions to cause you pain. I ask your forgiveness and assure you of my intention to change and to extend goodwill to you."

- "I want to make an amend to you about _____. For all those words that were said out of _____ (fear, thought-lessness, etc.) and confusion, I ask your forgiveness. I extend my promise of love and caring toward you."

AMENDS TO SELF GUIDELINES

The following are some guidelines to use when making amends to yourself.

Attitude

- Be willing to love and forgive yourself.
- Know what you want to say and take responsibility for your actions.
- Have reasonable expectations of yourself.
- Be willing to turn your anxieties over to your Higher Power.

Preparation

- Devote time to prayer and meditation.
- Delay the amend if you are angry or upset.
- Keep it simple. Explanations are not necessary.
- Remember the amend is to yourself and does not pertain to others.

Sample Amends

- "I was _____ (scared, overwhelmed, feeling abandoned, etc.) when _____ happened. I forgive myself for the _____ (harm done) and anything else I may have done in the past through my thoughts, words, or actions to cause myself harm."
- "I want to make an amend to myself about _____. I forgive myself for all the words that I said out of _____ (fear, thoughtlessness, etc.) and confusion."

Continued to take personal inventory and, when we were wrong, promptly admitted it.

Understanding Step Ten

Anyone who has planted a garden knows the care required to keep it healthy. We must remove the rocks and weeds, enrich the soil with fertilizer, bank it to hold water, plant the seeds, water, and guard against insects. Constant care is required to keep the garden clear of weeds, which could retake the garden if allowed. The garden once belonged to those weeds, and they always seem to want it back.

Our recovery is similar to a garden. Our lives once belonged to the weeds, our self-defeating behavior, but God has helped us plant a garden in our lives, pulled the weeds and caused some wonderful things to grow in their place. God used the Steps as tools and raised us to a place where things are different. We are beginning to see the promise of fruit, the promise of lasting change. In the midst of this new garden, we can also see the return of weeds. They don't die easily. In fact, as long as we live, weeds, our old self-defeating ways, will seek to recapture our lives. For that reason we must be ever vigilant to work Step Ten. We must continue to take personal inventory and protect our garden.

Working Step Ten

Step Ten is really a summary of Steps Four through Nine. We take an inventory of our lives and admit what we find. We become willing to have our Higher Power change us, and then we humbly ask God to remove the shortcomings. We make note of the amends needed and make those amends. The new element in Step Ten is the periodic inventory. We need to set aside regular times for personal inventory.

Preparing for Step Ten

We best prepare for Step Ten by scheduling time for our inventory. Setting aside time is important, or we may tend to avoid taking an inventory. We might plan for our inventory by setting aside a portion of our daily devotional or journal time. An option is allowing time during lunch or just before bedtime. A more extensive inventory can be made by spending a weekend at a retreat center each quarter or twice a year. Whatever the interval of time, the key is committing to take a regular inventory.

Prayer for Step Ten

Tenth Step Prayer

I pray I may continue:
To grow in understanding and effectiveness;
To take daily spot check inventories of myself;
To correct mistakes when I make them;
To take responsibility for my actions;
To be ever aware of my negative and self-defeating attitudes and To keep my willfulness in check;
To always remember I need your help;
To keep love and tolerance of others as my code; and
To continue in daily prayer how I can best serve you, my Higher Power.

(Taken from *12 Step Prayers for A Way Out,* page 75)

In Step Ten, we begin the maintenance part of the Steps. We will learn how to sustain what we have accomplished, become more confident, and proceed with joy along our spiritual journey. The first nine steps put our house in order and enabled us to change some of our destructive behaviors. This journey requires that we continue to rely on our Higher Power for guidance. Our work is beginning to pay off when we increase our capacity to develop new and healthier ways of taking care of ourselves and relating to others.

Some of us may wonder if the peace and serenity we are experiencing in our lives is permanent or just temporary. Working the steps has helped us to see how fragile and vulnerable we are. But with daily practice of the steps and with our Higher Power's loving presence in our lives, we will be able to achieve and maintain our newfound balance. Our relating skills will improve, and we will see how our interactions with others assume a new quality.

At this point, we may be tempted to revert to our old bravado and believe we are healed. We may think we have all the answers and can stop here. We feel comfortable with ourselves and see no need to continue with the program. We allow other activities to interfere and find excuses for skipping meetings and abandoning the program. We must resist this temptation to quit and realize that giving in will deprive us of realizing the goal we set for ourselves. Our successes can be maintained only if we are willing to depend upon God and practice the principles of the steps daily for the rest of our lives.

Step Ten points the way toward continued spiritual growth. In the past, we were constantly burdened by the results of our inattention to what we were doing. We allowed small problems to become large by ignoring them until they multiplied. Through our lack of sensitivity and skills to improve our behavior, we allowed our ineffective behavior to create havoc in our lives. In Step Ten, we consciously examine our daily conduct and admit our wrongs where necessary. We look at ourselves, see our errors, promptly admit them, and seek God's guidance in correcting them.

While we are working so carefully to monitor our actions and reactions, we must not judge ourselves too harshly. If we do, we face the possibility of returning to our negative attitudes. We need to recognize that nurturing ourselves emotionally and spiritually requires daily vigilance, loving understanding, and patience. Life is never stagnant; it is constantly changing, and each change requires adjustment and growth.

A personal inventory is a daily examination of our strengths and weaknesses, motives and behaviors. Taking daily inventory is not a time-consuming task and can usually be accomplished within fifteen minutes. When done with discipline and regularity, this is a small price to pay for continuing the good work we have begun.

It's important to monitor ourselves for signs that we are returning to our old attitudes and patterns of behavior. We may be attempting to manage our lives alone, manipulating others, or slipping into old patterns of resentment, dishonesty, or selfishness. When we see these temptations arising, we must immediately ask our Higher Power to forgive us, then make amends where needed. Daily practice of Step Ten maintains our honesty and humility and allows us to continue our development.

We become more conscious of our strengths and weaknesses when we examine our behaviors by taking regular inventory. We are less inclined to yield to feelings of anger, loneliness, and self-righteousness when we are emotionally balanced. Our personal inventory helps us discover who we are, what we are, and where we are going. We become more focused and better prepared to live the life we desire.

PERSONAL REFLECTION

The Twelve-Step program emphasizes the need for taking a regular personal inventory because many of us haven't developed the basic tools for self-appraisal. In time, we will appreciate the value of personal inventory. Although Step Ten inventories require some time and energy, the results are worth the effort. Three types of inventories are recommended; each serves a different purpose. These are Spot-Check Inventory, Daily Inventory, and Long-Term Periodic Inventory.

Spot-Check Inventory

A spot-check inventory involves stopping several times each day to assess our behavior and attitude. It is a short review of our actions, thoughts, and motives. This review can be useful in calming stormy emotions and it keeps us in touch with our behavior. It is a chance for examining situations, seeing where we are wrong, and taking prompt corrective action. Taking frequent inventories and immediately admitting our wrongs keeps us free from guilt and supports our spiritual growth. It is a good way to keep our lives free from anger, resentment, and unforgiveness.

Daily Inventory

It is important to stop at the end of each day or start at the beginning of the next and review what has happened. We should examine our lives daily to remind ourselves that this program is lived one day at a time. This action, with God's guidance, keeps us focused on the present and prevents us from worrying about the future or living in the past. It is an opportunity to keep in touch with our thoughts, feelings, and actions on a daily basis.

The daily inventory can be viewed as a balance sheet for the day—a summary of the good and the bad. It is an opportunity to reflect on our interactions with other people, things that happened, and a reminder of the difficulties we encountered. In the situations where we did well, we can feel good and acknowledge our progress. In those situations where we tried and failed, we need to acknowledge our attempt because we did try. We can then make amends and move forward with peace of mind. As we work the program, we can be assured that our number of successes will continue to increase.

Future situations may arise that will challenge our integrity and commitment. We need to be as honest and clear about our intentions as possible. Taking a few minutes to review our Step Four inventory can provide helpful insights to our recovery. Things to consider are:

- If we are isolating and feeling withdrawn, we need to reach out and share our difficulties with a friend.

- If we are slipping back, trying to control and manipulate others, we need to recognize this and ask our Higher Power to correct it.

- If we are comparing ourselves to others and feeling inferior, we need to reach out to supportive friends. We can then honestly examine our feelings to renew our own sense of self-worth.

- If we are becoming obsessive or compulsive and not taking care of ourselves, we need to stop and ask our Higher Power for help. We need to decide what unmet needs we are trying to fulfill and understand how to meet these needs.

- If we are fearing authority figures, we need to find the reason for our fear, acknowledge it, and ask our Higher Power for help.

- If we are depressed, we need to discover the central issue causing us to feel withdrawn or sorry for ourselves.

- If we are repressing our feelings, we need to take the necessary risks and express our feelings assertively.

Long-Term Periodic Inventory

A long-term periodic inventory can be accomplished by being alone or going away for a time. These are special days that can be set aside for reflection on our lives. We might attend a retreat or find a place of solitude. This is an important time that provides an opportunity for us to renew our intention to live healthier and more fulfilling lives.

This inventory can be done once or twice a year and will give us a chance to reflect on our progress. We will have an opportunity to see the remarkable changes we have made and to renew our hope and courage. We must be careful not to inflate our ego and must remind ourselves that our progress is a product of God's help and careful spiritual growth. Long-term inventories help us recognize problem areas in our lives. These inventories enable us to get a larger perspective of our behavior and allow us the chance to make significant changes. During these special inventories, we will discover new defects as well as new strengths.

If we sincerely want to change our lifestyle, we take personal inventory regularly and continue to interact with others in recovery. This reminds us that we are not unique—that everyone gets upset occasionally and no one is always "right." Through this awareness, we develop the ability to be forgiving and understanding and to love others for who they are and where they are. By being kind, courteous, and fair, we will often receive the same in return and can expect to achieve harmony in many of our relationships.

As we progress in our recovery, we see how pointless it is to become angry or to allow others to inflict emotional pain on us. Taking periodic, regular inventory and promptly admitting our wrongs keeps us from harboring resentments and allows us to maintain our dignity and respect for ourselves and others.

The conscientious practice of Step Ten has many benefits; most importantly, it strengthens and protects our recovery. Step Ten keeps us from returning to old patterns or behaviors such as:

- Medicating any discomfort through alcohol or drugs
- Distracting ourselves through compulsive behaviors such as eating or shopping
- Hiding from life through isolation
- Denying our needs through control and manipulation of others
- Escaping reality through fantasies
- Soothing our low self-esteem through people pleasing

Working the steps is a way for us to develop a daily discipline that deepens our love for God and enables us to be genuinely sorry for our wrongs. It helps us in continually striving for improvement in our relationships with our Higher Power and others. Learning to face our faults daily and correct them promptly provides God with the opportunity to mold our character and lifestyle. Delay in admitting our wrongs shows a resistance to working Step Ten. This is harmful and will only make matters worse.

The ongoing practice of Step Ten has many rewards, such as:

- Our relationship problems diminish. Taking inventory and admitting our wrongs promptly dissolves many misunderstandings without further incident.
- We learn to express ourselves and not fear being "found out." We see that, by being honest, we do not need to hide behind a false front.

- We no longer have to pretend we are flawless and can be candid about admitting our wrongs.

- Through admitting our own wrongs, others may become aware of their own behavior difficulties. We develop a better understanding of others and can express ourselves honestly.

KEY IDEAS

Personal Inventory: The Step Ten personal inventory is much like the moral inventory in Step Four. The difference is the ongoing and frequent nature of the Step Ten inventory. The idea of "personal" is a reminder to us that the inventory process is about us, not others.

Spot-Check Inventory: The spot-check inventory is the most frequent self-check. Through this inventory we monitor our actions throughout the day. We might designate objects or times in our day as reminders. For example, a red dot on our desk calendar might serve as a reminder to take a spot-check inventory. Or a prayer taped to our refrigerator might help us remember.

Daily Inventory: Quality time every day needs to be set aside for our daily inventory. This can be a few minutes before bed or early in the morning when our minds are clear. It is best to use a journal or inventory log for this daily inventory. This will serve as a reminder that progress is being made—one day at a time.

Long-Term Periodic Inventory: The long-term periodic inventory is done after a longer period of time. We may take this inventory every quarter, twice a year, or annually—the specific interval is not important. The idea is to occasionally get away and take a thorough inventory that reflects upon longer periods of time. In this way we are able to view patterns and seasons in our lives. If possible, it is helpful to find some form of retreat or solitude for this inventory.

IMPORTANT GUIDELINES IN EVALUATING PERSONAL GROWTH

The material offered in this guide is intended to help you evaluate your personal growth. The material includes feelings and behaviors from the Step Four inventory exercise. They are presented again to provide you with the opportunity to evaluate your progress in these important areas.

When doing this inventory, choose the traits, feelings, or behaviors that specifically apply to you. Don't tackle them all at once. Use recent events and record words and actions as accurately as possible. Take your time. This process enables you to evaluate your growth. You are the primary beneficiary of your honesty and thoroughness in this inventory.

At the end of each character trait, feeling, or behavior is a self-evaluation exercise. This same exercise was used in Step Four. It is provided again as another opportunity to measure your growth.

RECOVERY FROM RESENTMENT

We experience a release from resentment when we begin to understand that those who mistreated us were also spiritually sick. We extend to them the tolerance and forgiveness that God gives us. When we concentrate on our own inventories in Step Four and Ten, we put the wrongs of others out of our mind, and we focus on our faults, not the faults of others.

As we recover from resentment, we begin to:
Feel tolerance for others   Forgive those who hurt us
Focus on our inventory   Accept some blame
Release the need to retaliate   Feel compassion for others

Consider specific examples of your behavior that show you overcoming resentment.

Self-evaluation: On a scale from one to ten, how much does resentment negatively affect your life? Number one indicates that it has little negative effect. Number ten indicates that it has great negative effect. Circle where you are today.

| 1 | 2 | 3 | 4 | 5 | 6 | 7 | 8 | 9 | 10 |

RECOVERY FROM FEAR

Fear becomes less of a problem for us as our faith in God grows. We list our fears one by one and consider why they have power over us. We especially note the fears that grow out of our failed self-reliance. God is able to manage where we could not. Our faith empowers us to release our need for self-reliance and the fear that goes with it.

As we recover from fear, we begin to:

Feel less threatened   Embrace change
Rely on God   Face our fear honestly
Feel more joy   Pray more

Consider specific examples of your behavior that show you are less fearful.

Self-evaluation: On a scale from one to ten, how much does fear negatively affect your life? Number one indicates that it has little negative effect. Number ten indicates that it has great negative effect. Circle where you are today.

| 1 | 2 | 3 | 4 | 5 | 6 | 7 | 8 | 9 | 10 |

RECOVERY FROM REPRESSED OR INAPPROPRIATE ANGER

Learning to express anger appropriately is a major step in our recovery. It releases many hidden emotions and allows healing to take place. Expressing anger lets others know our limits and helps us to be honest with ourselves. As we learn to express anger more appropriately, we are better able to cope with our own hostility and also the anger of others. Our relationships improve as we begin to feel comfortable expressing ourselves. Stress-related problems diminish, and we even feel better physically.

As we recover from repressed or inappropriate anger, we begin to:

Express anger appropriately   Set limits for ourselves
Identify hurt feelings   Enjoy inner peace
Make reasonable requests   Reduce stress and anxiety

Consider specific examples of your behavior that show you can express anger in a healthy way.

Self-evaluation: On a scale from one to ten, how much does repressed or inappropriate anger negatively affect your life? Number one indicates that it has little negative effect. Number ten indicates that it has great negative effect. Circle where you are today.

| 1 | 2 | 3 | 4 | 5 | 6 | 7 | 8 | 9 | 10 |

RECOVERY FROM APPROVAL SEEKING

As we begin to rely on our own approval and that of our Higher Power, we understand that wanting approval is OK, and we learn to ask for it and not manipulate others to get it. We accept compliments from others and learn to simply say "thank you," believing that the compliment is sincere. We say "yes" when it is a comfortable answer. We are willing to say "no" when "no" is appropriate.

As we recover from inappropriate approval seeking, we begin to:

Recognize our own needs   Be loyal to ourselves
Tell the truth about how we feel   Build our confidence

Consider specific examples of your behavior that show you have experienced some recovery from inappropriate approval seeking.

Self-evaluation: On a scale from one to ten, how much does approval seeking negatively affect your life? Number one indicates that it has little negative effect. Number ten indicates that it has great negative effect. Circle where you are today.

| 1 | 2 | 3 | 4 | 5 | 6 | 7 | 8 | 9 | 10 |

RECOVERY FROM CARETAKING

As we put aside the role of caretaker, we assume less responsibility for everyone and everything and we allow individuals to find their own way. We give them over to the care of their Higher Power, which is the best source for their guidance, love, and support. By dropping the burden of meeting everyone's needs, we find time to develop our own personalities. Our obsession with caring for others is replaced by an acceptance of the fact that ultimately we have no power over the lives of others. We realize that our main responsibility in life is for our own welfare and happiness. We turn other people over to God's care.

When we stop being caretakers, we begin to:

Stop rescuing others   Develop our own identity
Take care of ourselves   Recognize dependent
                                  relationships

Consider specific examples of your behavior that show you are lessening your role as caretaker.

Self-evaluation: On a scale from one to ten, how much does caretaking negatively affect your life? Number one indicates that it has little negative effect. Number ten indicates that it has great negative effect. Circle where you are today.

| 1 | 2 | 3 | 4 | 5 | 6 | 7 | 8 | 9 | 10 |

RECOVERY FROM CONTROL

As we become more aware of the ways we have attempted to control people and things, we begin to realize that our efforts have been useless. We did not control anything or anyone except ourselves. We discover more effective ways to get our needs met when we start accepting God as the source of our security. As we begin to surrender our wills and our lives to God's care, we will experience less stress and anxiety. We become more able to participate in activities without being primarily concerned with the outcome. Saying the Serenity Prayer is helpful whenever we begin to recognize the reappearance of our need for control.

As we learn to give up control, we begin to:

Accept change	Reduce our stress levels
Trust in ourselves	Find ways to have fun
Empower others	Accept others as they are

Consider specific examples of your behavior that show you feel less of a need to be in control.

Self-evaluation: On a scale from one to ten, how much does controlling negatively affect your life? Number one indicates that it has little negative effect. Number ten indicates that it has great negative effect. Circle where you are today.

| 1 | 2 | 3 | 4 | 5 | 6 | 7 | 8 | 9 | 10 |

RECOVERY FROM
FEAR OF ABANDONMENT

As we learn to rely more upon the ever-present love of God, our confidence in life and the future increases. Our fear of abandonment diminishes and is replaced by the feeling that we are worthy people in our own right. We seek out healthy relationships with people who love and take care of themselves. We feel more secure in revealing our feelings. We transfer our old dependence on others to trust in God. We learn to understand and accept a nurturing and loving fellowship within our community. Our self-confidence grows as we begin to realize that with God in our lives, we will never again be totally alone.

As fear of abandonment diminishes, we begin to:

Be honest about feelings Reduce our caretaking
Consider our own needs   Feel comfortable
 in a relationship   being alone

Consider specific examples of your behavior that show your fear of abandonment is decreasing.

Self-evaluation: On a scale from one to ten, how much does fear of abandonment negatively affect your life? Number one indicates that it has little negative effect. Number ten indicates that it has great negative effect. Circle where you are today.

| 1 | 2 | 3 | 4 | 5 | 6 | 7 | 8 | 9 | 10 |

RECOVERY FROM FEAR
OF AUTHORITY FIGURES

As we begin to feel comfortable with people in roles of authority, we learn to put our focus on ourselves and discover that we have nothing to fear. We recognize others to be like us, with their own fears, defenses, and insecurities. Others' behavior no longer dictates how we feel about ourselves. We start acting and not reacting when responding to others. We recognize that our ultimate authority figure is God and that God is always with us.

As we become comfortable with authority figures, we begin to:

Act with increased self-esteem   Experience less fear
Accept constructive criticism   Interact easily with
Stand up for ourselves   people in authority

Consider specific examples of your behavior that show you are gaining confidence around people in authority.

Self-evaluation: On a scale from one to ten, how much does fear of authority figures negatively affect your life? Number one indicates that it has little negative effect. Number ten indicates that it has great negative effect. Circle where you are today.

| 1 | 2 | 3 | 4 | 5 | 6 | 7 | 8 | 9 | 10 |

RECOVERY FROM FROZEN FEELINGS

As we get in touch with our feelings and learn to express them, strange things begin to happen. Our stress levels decrease as we become able to express ourselves honestly, and we begin to see ourselves as worthy. We learn that expression of true feelings is the healthy way to communicate, and we find that more of our own needs are being met. All we have to do is ask. As we begin to release our feelings, we experience some levels of pain. But, as our courage increases, the pain goes away, and we develop a sense of peace and serenity. The more willing we are to take risks in releasing our emotions, the more effective our recovery will be.

As we experience and express our feelings, we begin to:

Feel free to cry   Experience our true self
Feel healthier   Express our needs to others

Consider specific examples of your behavior that show you are becoming aware of your feelings and are able to express them more easily.

Self-evaluation: On a scale from one to ten, how much do frozen feelings negatively affect your life? Number one indicates that they have little negative effect. Number ten indicates that they have great negative effect. Circle where you are today.

| 1 | 2 | 3 | 4 | 5 | 6 | 7 | 8 | 9 | 10 |

RECOVERY FROM IRRESPONSIBILITY

As we understand that God will help us achieve realistic goals, we begin to work in partnership with God for our future. We place less value on the expectations others have of us and more value on our own desires to achieve goals in life. We understand that we are competing only with ourselves, and God will enable us to do what is needed to win at life. God brings order to our lives as we surrender control, and makes it possible for us to contribute in meaningful ways.

As we recover from irresponsibility, we begin to:

Keep commitments   Accept responsibilities
Set goals for ourselves   Feel better about ourselves

Consider specific examples of your behavior that show you are less irresponsible.

Self-evaluation: On a scale from one to ten, how much does irresponsibility negatively affect your life? Number one indicates that it has little negative effect. Number ten indicates that it has great negative effect. Circle where you are today.

| 1 | 2 | 3 | 4 | 5 | 6 | 7 | 8 | 9 | 10 |

RECOVERY FROM ISOLATION

As we begin to feel better about ourselves, we become more willing to take risks and expose ourselves to new surroundings. We seek friends and relationships that are nurturing, safe, and supportive. We learn to participate and to have fun in group activities. It becomes easier to express our feelings as we develop a stronger sense of self-esteem. We recognize that people will accept us for who we really are. Our self-acceptance allows us to experience the precious gift of living more comfortably and serenely.

As we isolate less often, we begin to:
Accept ourselves   Cultivate supportive
Freely express our emotions   relationships
Actively participate with others

Consider specific examples of your behavior that show you isolate yourself less frequently.

Self-evaluation: On a scale from one to ten, how much does isolation negatively affect your life? Number one indicates that it has little negative effect. Number ten indicates that it has great negative effect. Circle where you are today.

| 1 | 2 | 3 | 4 | 5 | 6 | 7 | 8 | 9 | 10 |

RECOVERY FROM LOW SELF-ESTEEM

As we work with our Higher Power to build confidence in ourselves and our abilities, our self-esteem increases. We are able to interact with others and accept ourselves as we really are. We see our strengths as well as our limitations. We learn to accept ourselves at face value. We become more willing to take risks, and we realize we can achieve many things that we had never dreamed possible. Sharing feelings with others becomes more comfortable. We feel safer as we come to know others and allow them to know us. Relationships become healthier because we are able to trust and validate ourselves. We no longer need to look to others for validation.

As our self-esteem increases, we begin to:

Be more confident	Love ourselves
Act more assertively	Openly express feelings
Easily interact with others	Take risks

Consider specific examples of your behavior that show your self-esteem is improving.

Self-evaluation: On a scale from one to ten, how much does low self-esteem negatively affect your life? Number one indicates that it has little negative effect. Number ten indicates that it has great negative effect. Circle where you are today.

| 1 | 2 | 3 | 4 | 5 | 6 | 7 | 8 | 9 | 10 |

RECOVERY FROM OVERDEVELOPED SENSE OF RESPONSIBILITY

Accepting the fact that we are not responsible for the actions and feelings of others forces us to focus on ourselves. We understand that we can't force others to change and that people are responsible for themselves. As we assume responsibility for our own actions, we become aware that we must rely on God for guidance and take care of our own needs. Then we will find time and energy to support and nurture ourselves.

As we stop being too responsible, we begin to:

Take care of ourselves   Accept our limitations
Enjoy leisure time   Delegate responsibility

Consider specific examples of your behavior that show you are feeling less responsible for others.

Self-evaluation: On a scale from one to ten, how much does overdeveloped sense of responsibility negatively affect your life? Number one indicates that it has little negative effect. Number ten indicates that it has great negative effect. Circle where you are today.

| 1 | 2 | 3 | 4 | 5 | 6 | 7 | 8 | 9 | 10 |

RECOVERY FROM INAPPROPRIATELY EXPRESSED SEXUALITY

As we rely upon the constant love of our Higher Power, our self-worth increases, and we see ourselves as worthy. As we increase our self-love and our ability to take care of ourselves, we seek to be with other healthy people who love and take care of themselves. We fear commitment less and are better prepared to enter a healthy relationship—emotionally, intellectually, and sexually. We feel more secure in sharing our feelings, strengths, and weaknesses. Our self-confidence grows and allows us to be vulnerable. We give up the need for perfection in ourselves and others and, in so doing, open ourselves to growth and change. We are honest about our own sexuality with our children. We accept their need for information and also their need for a healthy sexual identity.

When we accept our sexuality, we begin to:

Discuss sex openly   Share intimate feelings
Accept our sexual self   Consider our own
                              sexual needs

Consider specific examples of how you are becoming comfortable with your sexuality.

Self-evaluation: On a scale from one to ten, how much does inappropriately expressed sexuality negatively affect your life? Number one indicates that it has little negative effect. Number ten indicates that it has great negative effect. Circle where you are today.

| 1 | 2 | 3 | 4 | 5 | 6 | 7 | 8 | 9 | 10 |

STEP ELEVEN

Sought through prayer and meditation to improve our conscious contact with God as we understood God, praying only for knowledge of God's will for us and the power to carry that out.

Understanding Step Eleven

Vital to a healthy relationship is honest communication and a willingness to be ourselves. If partners choose not to talk honestly with each other, their relationship will suffer in every area and may eventually fail. On the other hand, when communication and honesty exist, relationships are strengthened, and broken relationships can be healed.

Our relationship with our Higher Power is our most important asset, and it is impossible without communication. As we draw nearer to our Higher Power in prayer and meditation, we draw closer to our source of power, serenity, guidance, and healing. To ignore the need to communicate with God is to unplug our power source.

Working Step Eleven

We work Step Eleven through the routine practice of prayer and meditation. Through prayer we talk to God. Through meditation we listen to God. Many of us, however, struggle with the idea of prayer and meditation as a way to maintain contact with our Higher Power. We know prayers, but we don't know how to pray. Many of us may be unfamiliar with meditation and resistant to trying it.

Step Eleven is communicating with God. It is the work of learning the intimacy and power of prayer and meditation. It is the act of seeking our Higher Power's will for us.

Preparing for Step Eleven

We prepare for Step Eleven by taking prayer and meditation seriously. Many of us have a tendency to put prayer and meditation on the second shelf, to treat both as unimportant or unnecessary. We need to prepare for this step by developing an understanding appreciation for prayer and meditation. If we struggle in this area, we might counsel with a therapist, talk with an experienced program member, or otherwise seek help and insight from a close friend.

Prayer for Step Eleven

Eleventh Step Prayer

Higher Power, as I understand you,

I pray to keep my connection with you open and clear from the confusion of daily life. Through my prayers and meditations I ask especially for freedom from self-will, retaionalization, and wishful thinking. I pray for the guidance of correct thought and positive action. Your will, Higher Power, not mine, be done.

(Taken from *12 Step Prayers for A Way Out*, page 82)

Steps Ten and Eleven are the tools that help us trust God more fully and sustain the progress we have made in Steps One through Nine. In the first three steps, we recognized the seriousness of our condition and established the foundation for dealing with our problems. In Steps Four through Nine, we experienced a process similar to that of taking our car to the garage for a long-overdue, major overhaul. We devoted the time and energy required to make the necessary repairs and restore our "engine" to its proper running condition. In Steps Ten and Eleven, we have the opportunity to keep ourselves in tune by devoting time to regular service and maintenance. As we continue in this direction, we learn to recognize problems, to correct them promptly, and to continually seek guidance from our Higher Power. This enhances our ability to improve our new skills for living life to the fullest. If we provide the required maintenance, we will find that our lives will run smoothly.

Step Eleven requires that we improve our conscious contact with God, as we understand God. To do this, we need to be consistent, patient, and willing to practice. We have made contact with God in three of the earlier Steps. In Step Three, we made a decision to turn our will and our lives over to God's care. In Step Five, we admitted our wrongs directly to God. In Step Seven, we humbly asked God to help us remove our shortcomings. Step Eleven gives us a means of strengthening that contact and enables us to bring our Higher Power into our daily lives. Now we can let go of our feelings of aloneness and alienation and enjoy the quality partnership that is truly life-giving and life-sustaining. It is in Step Eleven that we have an opportunity to exercise the discipline of daily prayer and meditation.

Through the progress we have made in working the steps, we are learning more about what we want to achieve in the program. To protect what we have learned, we must continually seek to know God's will for us. A daily regimen of prayer and meditation makes it clear that relief from pain of the past is just a day-to-day reprieve. We must relentlessly seek to know God's will for us and how we are to live our lives.

Those of us who have experienced the hell and chaos caused by our willful acts realize that we worshiped false gods such as drugs, sex, money, or addictive relationships. We may have suffered severe losses as a result of our behavior. Surrendering to the Twelve-Step process was not the step that led us to heaven, but was, in fact, the step that led us out of the hell that our lives had become.

Spiritual growth and development occur slowly and only through discipline and reliance upon God. As our self-esteem increases and our Higher Power becomes a trusted friend, we grow more confident in the fact that God is with us, especially when we pray. And we grow more confident that God's will is what we want for our lives.

Our intention to do God's will can sometimes be compromised by the appearance of our old behaviors. As we experience this struggle on a daily basis, the need for help from our Higher Power becomes evident. In Step Eleven, we focus on deepening our relationship with our Higher Power. It is mostly through our quiet moments of prayer and meditation that the presence and guidance of a Higher Power becomes clear to us. As our relationship with our Higher Power improves, we see how we can rely and depend upon that Power for courage and strength in meeting life's challenges. We may experience a spiritual awakening that comes when we are willing and able to acknowledge, from the depth of our being, that a Higher Power can and will direct our lives.

Note: Before proceeding, refer to Guidelines for Prayer and Meditation on page 151.

PERSONAL REFLECTION

How do we pray and for what do we pray? Many of us were taught to pray before we understood what it meant. In the beginning, we may have use the prayer "Now I lay me down to sleep,..." or asked God to bless Mommy and Daddy and others who were close to us. As we grew, our hurtful family experiences brought us great pain; those we depended upon hurt and disappointed us. Perhaps we blamed God for not hearing and answering our desperate prayers. Based on the program principles, our attitudes toward prayer change as we work the Steps. We learn to ask that God's will for our lives be shown to us, trusting that our best interests will be served. The old habit of praying for material things will diminish, to be replaced with prayers for guidance. We begin to rely upon some of the slogans and prayers, such as "Let Go and Let God" or The Serenity Prayer. Our prayers can be simple sentence prayers, such as *"God, please help me,"* or *"Thank you, Higher Power."* God will hear and respond to our most humble call for aid.

Spending time in meditation enables us to become better acquainted with God in the same way that we become better acquainted with someone we would really like to know. Meditation can be difficult at first. We are accustomed to being active and may feel uncomfortable with sitting still and calming our busy thoughts. We may feel we are wasting time, instead of doing something more productive than sitting quietly, reflecting on the events of the day and inviting God to share our experiences with us. Actually, nothing could be more productive.

In the act of meditating, we ponder and apply our knowledge of God's ways to our daily lives. It is contemplation done in the presence of and with the help of God. It is two-way communion with him. Meditation's purpose is to clear our mental and spiritual vision and to let God's truth make its full and proper impact on our minds and hearts. Meditation humbles us as we contemplate God's greatness and glory and allow ourselves to be encouraged, reassured, and comforted by God's presence.

In developing a routine for prayer and meditation, we seek times and places to invite God's presence. Our desire

is to be available for him. Some simple guidelines for learning to pray and meditate are:

- Pray and meditate in solitude. Be alone and undisturbed,
  so you can be totally free from distractions.

- Pray and meditate in silence, or talk quietly to God without
  interruptions. Outside influences disrupt your concen-
  tration and inhibit your ability to tell God your thoughts
  and feelings.

- Set aside quality time. Do not wait until you are tired
  or your ability to clear your mind is hindered.

- Listen carefully. God has messages for you, just as you
  have messages for God.

- Review your daily inventory with your Higher Power.
  Admit your wrongs, ask for forgiveness, and make amends
  as needed.

- End your session by asking for knowledge of God's will
  for you and the power to carry it out.

If we are progressing with Step Eleven by praying and
meditating daily, we will see positive signs. We will feel
more at peace in our daily affairs. We will experience a
new sense of security and a deep sense of gratitude for
our ongoing healing. We will feel as though we have finally
achieved a rightful place in the world. Feelings of self-worth
will replace feelings of shame. Friends and family members
will notice a change in us. These signs tell us that God is
guiding and sustaining our recovery.

When we combine prayer and meditation with self-examination, we discover the secret to successfully working
the steps. We also discover an effective means for main-
taining a rewarding spiritual life. No matter how dedicated
we are to recovery, we all have moments of doubt about
the direction of our lives. We may even question the need

to continue working the steps or attending support group meetings. Sometimes, we are tempted to regress to our old compulsive behavior. We are especially vulnerable when we feel pressured for accomplishment or when we expect events to follow our own time schedule. In our frustration, we often tend to seize control from God's hands and attempt to hasten the process through our own willfulness. When we do this, we are not following God's guidance and must renew the commitment we made in Step Three.

Methods of prayer and meditation may vary. Whatever our style is, it is our desire to hear and feel heard that counts. Our primary commitment is to deepen our relationship and expand our communication with our Higher Power. This means being honest about our feelings and thoughts, admitting our limitations, and bringing our failings to God for forgiveness. Through a faithful and disciplined dedication to prayer and meditation, we become aware of God's unconditional love, forgiveness, and constant presence in our lives. If we continue to pray with patience and trust, we will be rewarded with endless gifts of peace, serenity, love, and joy.

Routine practice of prayer and meditation give us an opportunity to ask for knowledge of God's plan for us, and the power to carry it out. God gave us intellect and free will, through which we have the ability to think and act. When practicing Step Eleven, we must not create excuses to delay our actions or rationalize that we are "waiting" for God's will. Part of doing God's will is taking action and trusting that our Higher Power is working through us.

In unclear situations, it is sometimes wise to seek outside counsel. As God continues to reach out to us in different ways, revelations may come to us through other people or new experiences. After careful review of the situation, our guidance may be obvious and compelling or still unclear. If unclear, we must be patient and wait for more direction to be revealed to us. If we cannot wait, we should select the best course of action and trust that God is with us, guiding us as we go. Our faith in our Higher Power's guidance will allow us to receive what needs to be revealed to us. The way we feel and function clearly shows if God's will is being done, or if we are trying to control the outcome.

If we place our will in God's care, and pray sincerely for guidance, we find ourselves trusting that our will is being redirected. We then experience the courage and power to act according to God's will for us. Seeking higher guidance is an experience in humility, because we are so accustomed to running our lives by our own plan and making demands on God to give us what we think we want. Our own desires and opinions are so much a part of us that we may, at times, view the will of a Higher Power as a manifestation of what we think should happen.

"PRAYER OF SAINT FRANCIS OF ASSISI"

Lord, make me an instrument of your peace!
Where there is hatred—let me sow love
Where there is injury—pardon
Where there is doubt—faith
Where there is despair—hope
Where there is darkness—light
Where there is sadness—joy
O Divine Master, grant that I may not so much seek
To be consoled—as to console
To be loved—as to love
for
It is in giving—that we receive
It is in pardoning—that we are pardoned
It is in dying—that
we are born to eternal life.
Amen

KEY IDEAS

Prayer: Prayer is communication with our Higher Power. And the most effective prayer is honest and frequent. Virtually every form of communication that we have with any other person is appropriate with our Higher Power. It is fitting to complain to God, to lament before God, to thank God, to share the details of our lives with God, to praise God, and to talk to God as we would talk to a trusted friend. The only inappropriate prayer in the Twelve Step program is the "wish-list" prayer in which we petition our Higher Power as though God were Santa Claus. Our major petition of God in this program is to know God's will for our lives.

Meditation: Meditation has often been called listening prayer because in meditation, we quiet our hearts, minds, and even our bodies so that our spirits might be opened to our Higher Power. Although meditation may have physical and mental elements, it is a spiritual exercise. The major challenge in meditation is the challenge that quiet or silence presents to us. Many of us are frightened by silence because when the noise of our lives ceases, the noise in our heads begins. That internal noise is called many things: the committee, shame, stinkin' thinkin', negative self-talk, etc. But the internal noise and pain can be so strong that some of us avoid silence and quiet at any cost. We prefer external noise, distracting activity, consuming relationships, even crisis above the quiet

The discipline and practice of meditation would have us systematically seek periods of quiet and face our internal noise. Once we face our internal noise we can admit our powerlessness over it, believe in God's ability to help us grow beyond it, and turn it over to our Higher Power.

Only then can we carve out a quiet center in our lives where we can meet with and hear our Higher Power.

Conscious Contact: For many years zealous believers of various faiths have used "prayer rocks" to remind themselves of their constant need for prayer. Tiny pebbles in their shoes reminded them in their every step to reach out to God. Fist-sized stones under their pillows prompted them to pray even as they retired to sleep. Although we may not agree that rocks in our shoes and beds are necessary to remind us to pray, we should agree that constant contact with our Higher Power is necessary. The Twelve Steps teach us that our very best thinking and effort isn't enough. We need the daily help and support of our Higher Power. We learn that life is best lived in small steps—one day at a time, or sometimes, one hour at a time. This ongoing contact with God throughout our daily lives is a must for our continued recover.

God's Will: Before any building, highway, or development is physically constructed, an architect develops a detailed plan for the project. From the architect's plans and blueprints, the builders and workers can do the work required. In a similar sense, we realize that our Higher Power is the preferred architect for our own lives. God's will for our lives is the plan we desire to follow. We use prayer and meditation to get God's blueprint or will for each new day as it comes. In the past, when we followed our own plans, the structures of our lives were poorly constructed and dangerous. But today, with our Higher Power providing the plans, the structures of our lives are straight and strong and we are able to withstand the earthquakes that life brings.

GUIDELINES FOR PRAYER AND MEDITATION

The wisdom and guidance experienced through the practice of Step Eleven is available to us any time of the day or night. The steps are useful tools for us wherever we are in our spiritual journey. An overview of prayer and meditation for a given day may be outlined as follows:

At the beginning of the day, review your plans and:

- Ask God for direction in your thoughts and actions, to keep you free from self-pity, dishonesty, or self-righteousness.

- Ask your Higher Power to provide the guidance needed to take care of any problems.

- Pray for freedom from self-will and selfishness.

During the day, in moments of indecision or fear:

- Ask God for inspiration and guidance.

- Reflect on Step Three and turn it over.

- Notice feelings of tension or stress in your body and identify what you can do that is both nurturing and relaxing.

- Pray to your Higher Power as often as necessary during the day, even if the prayer is as short as "God, please help me, I feel _____ (fear, panic, out of control)."

- Make contact with a support person to identify and share what is happening.

At the end of the day, review the events that happened and:

- Review Step Ten and take a personal inventory.

- Ask God for guidance in taking corrective action.

- Pray for knowledge of your Higher Power's will for you.

- Ask God's forgiveness where needed, and acknowledge that this review is not intended to cause obsessive thinking, worry, remorse, or morbid reflection.

- Give thanks to your Higher Power for the guidance and blessings that were part of the day.

STEP TWELVE

Having had a spiritual awakening as the result of these Steps, we tried to carry this message to others, and to practice these principles in all our affairs.

Understanding Step Twelve

In most every house with children there is a certain wall or a doorpost with pencil marks. These pencil marks, which have dates or ages next to them, keep track of growth. Every few months the kids back up against the wall while mom or dad mark their height. Sometimes the growth is barely noticeable and other times the growth is drastic.

Step Twelve is a time for noticing growth. Through God's goodness and our commitment to work the steps, we have had a life-changing spiritual experience. We began this journey as frightened tyrants clinging to control our own little kingdoms. But we end this round of our journey with a new king on the throne: God. Although we know we have grown through this process, the mark on the wall is a little shorter—it's minus the crown.

Working Step Twelve

Step Twelve involves taking time to appreciate the spiritual growth in our lives. We work this step by sharing the program with others and continuing to practice the principles of the steps in every area of our lives.

Preparing for Step Twelve

We can prepare for Step Twelve by ensuring that our Higher Power has been a part of every aspect of our program. If we have merely added God as an ingredient to our recovery, we will not notice any spiritual awakening in Step Twelve. If we have kept control in our own hands, we will find no spiritual awakening now. However, the spiritual awakening of Step Twelve will be ours if we have done all of the following: relied upon our Higher Power's presence, worked the steps in partnership with God, and surrendered control of our will and lives.

Prayer for Step Twelve

Twelfth Step Prayer

Dear God,

My spiritual awakening continues to unfold. The help I have received I shall pass on and give to others, both in and out of the fellowship. For this opportunity I am grateful.

I pray most humbly to continue walking day by day on the road of spiritual progress. I pray for the inner strength and wisdom to practice the principles of this way of life in all I do and say. I need you, my friends, and the program every hour of every day. This is a better way to live.

(Taken from *12 Step Prayers for A Way Out,* page 92)

The Twelfth Step completes the climb of this particular mountain. Remembering the milestones during this adventure reminds us of the pain and joy we have experienced while accomplishing our objective. Our experiences have been unique and personal to each of us. We now realize that all the events of our lives have pulled together to show us our connection to God and the universe. Our spiritual awakening has changed us, so now we have the capacity to live our lives as an expression of God's will.

Step Twelve requires that we are instrumental in helping others receive God's message of hope and healing through working the Twelve Steps. Many of us were introduced to this program by someone who was working Step Twelve. Now we have the opportunity to promote our own growth by helping others. We look for ways to share our new confidence because of our commitment to recovery and our growing awareness of God's presence in our lives. This program calls us to live our program daily and explain to others the effectiveness of the Twelve-Step principles.

This step reminds us that we have not yet completed our journey to wholeness. To continue our process of growth, we need to be aware that we have just begun to learn the principles that will improve the quality of our lives. Each of the Twelve Steps is a vital part of fulfilling God's plan for us. When our daily challenges distract and separate us from our Higher Power, we can use the steps as tools for coping with our problems and drawing us back. Step One reminds us of our powerlessness. Steps Two and Three show us the ongoing need for God's help. Steps Four through Nine guide us through self-examination and making amends. Steps Ten and Eleven help us minimize our slips and keep us in touch with our Higher Power. We are blessed through our conscientious attention to seeking God's will and to working the steps. Our blessings may include a level of love, acceptance, honesty, and peace of mind that we never experienced before. The hardest part of any journey is the beginning, and this step is our milestone. By reaching Step Twelve, we have shown our commitment to God's will in our recovery.

Our spiritual awakening is a gift that instills in us a new perspective. It is usually accompanied by a significant change in our value system. Our pursuit of worldly goals has been subdued and redirected. We now look for fulfillment from things with real and lasting value. For most of us, the awakening is subtle and best seen in hindsight. It seldom has a distinct beginning and ending. We also realize it took hard work to get us here. As we awaken to the presence of our Higher Power's love for us, our lives become filled with new purpose and meaning.

PERSONAL REFLECTION

"Actions speak louder than words" is an accurate description of how we should carry the Twelve-Step message to others. It is more effective to witness a principle being applied than to hear lectures on theory alone. For example, sharing our own experiences of prayer and meditation has more meaning than simply lecturing and explaining why everyone should meditate and pray. Telling our story will help others recognize their need for a relationship with God and encourage the growth of our own humility. Carrying the message gives us an opportunity to describe the ways in which our Higher Power works through the Twelve Steps to transform our lives. Each day our life experiences remind us how we are renewed in our relationship with our Higher Power. Through our sharing, we can convey the message of our experience, strength, and hope.

Working with newcomers to the program can be very rewarding. Many of them are troubled, confused, and resentful. They need guidance and help to understand that God will strengthen and change them through their Twelve-Step work. Through their willingness and commitment, they will experience rewards and miracles that far outweigh their present pain. We can encourage newcomers to be gentle with themselves and to work the program one day at a time. This can be a growth experience for us. As we reflect on where we were when first introduced to the program, we see how far we have come. When carrying the message, we can emphasize an important point about our decision to join the program. We made the decision only after we suffered enough, were discouraged, were tired of hurting, and had "hit bottom."

Our relationship with God is the key to our success in everything, particularly in working the steps and applying the principles in our daily affairs. We cannot allow ourselves to drift into indifference and neglect our commitment to living according to the will of our Higher Power. Life constantly reminds us that we need to be prepared to face temptations and trials. But, with God's help, we can transform them into occasions for growth and comfort to ourselves and to those around us. We will never achieve peace and serenity without God's help and guidance.

Sometimes we become discouraged and lose sight of our progress. If this happens, we can compare our past to our present and ask ourselves:

- Are we less isolated and no longer afraid of people in authority?

- Have we stopped seeking approval from others and accepted ourselves as we really are?

- Are we more selective of the people with whom we develop relationships, and more able to keep our own identity while in a relationship?

- Have we developed the ability to express our feelings?

- Have we stopped trying to dominate others?

- Are we no longer behaving childishly by turning friends or spouses into protective parents and being too dependent?

- Have we become attentive to the needs of our inner child?

Affirmative answers show the extent of our progress toward a healthier and better way of living.

An important achievement in working the steps occurs when we become accustomed to "living" the steps. We do this by habitually taking a problem or concern through the steps, while acknowledging our need for God's support and guidance. The result is peace and serenity and a new confidence that we can deal directly with the problems. Any action we take is then guided by God's will and our honest appraisal of the consequences. We can act confidently and without fear.

At this point, we begin to identify the many areas of our lives that are being affected by working the Twelve Steps. Our success with handling new problems is linked to our willingness to thoughtfully take action, while remembering to let go and turn it over to God. Our faith grows as we learn to relinquish control and allow God to be the director of our lives. The process is gradual, regenerative, and never ending. We slowly become more Higher Power centered as we learn the true meaning of God's love, our surrender, and spiritual serenity.

As we may view our lives now, we are the pens through which the ink of our Higher Power flows to write the story of our lives. Our step work has contributed to our deeper contact with God. Sharing each other's experience, strength, and hope has enabled us to expand our faith in our Higher Power and experience unconditional love.

KEY IDEAS

Spiritual Awakening: The spiritual awakening that Step Twelve speaks of is a gradual change in the control of our lives. This change eventually produces a realization that we sincerely trust God and can depend on him. We also realize that this new trust and dependence brings a peace and serenity that we have never experienced before. We come to Step Twelve with confidence that God can be trusted, miracles do happen, and prayer works.

Carrying the Message: In Step Twelve we are encouraged to carry the message of the Twelve Steps to others. If we have read *The Big Book of Alcoholics Anonymous,* we realize that early program members always understood that they were carrying a spiritual message. The message we carry is that God can save us from our self-defeating behavior, from our despair, from our torment—God can save us from ourselves. We carry a spiritual message that only God is able to control our lives and heal us. We will live more productive and healthy lives if we yield to a power greater than ourselves.

TWELVE-STEP REVIEW

Identify a situation or condition in your life that is currently a source of resentment, fear, sadness, or anger. It may involve relationships (family, work, or sexual), work environment, health, or self-esteem. Write a concise statement describing the situation and identify your concern.

Use the following exercise to apply the principles of the Twelve Steps to the above situation or condition.

Step One: Describe the ways in which you are powerless in this situation. How does this situation show you the unmanageability of your life?

Step Two: How can your Higher Power restore you to sanity?

Step Three: Write an affirmation in which you state your decision to turn this situation over to God (e.g., I am no longer willing to fret over my boss's behavior. I decide now to turn my anxiety, my concerns, and my need for security over to God).

Step Four: What character defects have surfaced (e.g., fear of abandonment, control, approval seeking, obsessive/compulsive behavior, unexpressed feelings)?

Step Five: Admit your wrongs to God, to yourself, and to another person.

Step Six: Reflect upon your willingness to have God remove the character defects that have surfaced. Describe your willingness or reasons for not being willing to have them removed.

Step Seven: Write a prayer in which you humbly ask God to remove the specific shortcomings relating to this situation (You can be most humble when you are honest about your shortcomings and your needs).

Step Eight: Make a list of the persons you have harmed.

Step Nine: Describe how you intend to make the necessary amends.

Step Ten: Review the above to be sure that nothing has been overlooked. What new issues have surfaced that require attention?

Step Eleven: Take a moment for prayer or meditation, asking or knowledge of your Higher Power's will for you. What is your understanding of God's will for you in this situation?

Step Twelve: In this situation have you to sensed a spiritual awakening? Who is in charge now, you or God? Explain. (Your attitude and emotions are good indicators.)

APPENDIX ONE

MEETING FORMAT

Leader:

"Hello, and welcome to *The Twelve Steps for Adult Children* support group meeting. My name is _____ and I am your trusted servant for today's meeting. Please join me for a moment of silence, after which we will recite the Serenity Prayer."

"SERENITY PRAYER"

God, grant me the serenity
to accept the things I cannot change,
the courage to change the things I can,
and the wisdom to know the difference.

Reinhold Niebuhr

"We are a support group committed to creating a safe place for men and women to share their experience, strength, and hope with each other."

"As a fellowship of men and women recovering from behaviors that have affected us in our lives, our purpose is to grow spiritually and in our relationship with our Higher Power. We are here for our own benefit, to share our own experience, strength and hope with others. We are not here to talk about others, to condemn, criticize, or judge them. Our desire is to improve the quality of our lives as we apply what we learn from listening to and sharing with each other. Our hope is in the belief that we can succeed today in situations where we failed previously. As we place ourselves in the care of our Higher Power, our attitudes improve as we honestly, openly, and willingly look at who we are and engage in healthier behavior."

"I've asked _____ to read The Twelve Steps."

"I've asked _____ to read (Common Behavior Characteristics or Promises)".

"Many of the principles and traditions of Alcoholics Anonymous are used as part of the basis of our group. We respect the confidentiality and anonymity of each person here. Remember that whatever you hear at this meeting is shared with the trust and confidence that it will remain here. Who you see here, what is said here, when you leave here, let it stay here."

"We are self-supporting through our own contributions. We ask for your contribution at this time." (Take time for collection before continuing.)

"If you are new to a Twelve-Step support group, we offer you a special welcome and invite you to attend at least 6 meetings to give yourself a fair chance to decide if this group is for you. We encourage you to exchange phone numbers with other members for support between meetings. Phone lists, literature, and information on other recovery support groups will be available after the meeting. If you have any questions, please feel free to talk with me at the end of the meeting."

"Is there anyone here today for the first time? If so, please tell us your first name so we can greet you."

"We will now introduce ourselves by first name only. My name is _____."

"This meeting is a step study using *The Twelve Steps for Adult Children*. The Twelve Steps represent a spiritual discipline that can provide a way out of destructive behavior and an opportunity to improve our relationship with our Higher Power."

"Everyone is invited to share, but no one is obligated to do so."

"Today's meeting focuses on Step _____. We will read a portion of the chapter, after which we will begin our time of sharing. Please turn to page _____."

"Please keep your sharing focused on recent experiences and events. Focus on your personal experience, strength, and hope."

"Limit your sharing to 3 to 5 minutes. Allow everyone in the group to share once before you share a second time."

"Please...*no cross talk*. Cross talk occurs when individuals speak out of turn and interrupt one another. The group is disrupted, and focus is diverted from the individual whose turn it is to speak."

Closing:

"This is a fellowship of recovering adults and is intended to complement other Twelve-Step groups. You are encouraged to attend other Twelve-Step recovery support groups during the week to support your recovery journey."

"I've asked _____ to read Milestones in Recovery."

"Are there any announcements?"

"Reminder! What you hear at this meeting is confidential; leave it at this meeting! It is not for public disclosure or gossip. Please respect the privacy of those who have shared here today."

"Will everyone please clean up after themselves and help rearrange the room?"

"Will all who care to, stand and join me in closing with (The Lord's Prayer or Prayer of St. Francis of Assisi)?"

"KEEP COMING BACK, IT WORKS!"

NOTES TO FACILITATOR

• *Appendix One* contains review questions for writing or sharing on this step.

• Leader begins the sharing by telling his or her story as it pertains to the step being discussed. Allow per person a maximum of 10 minutes to share.

• If the group is larger than 20 people it is advisable to form small groups of 5 to 7 people for the sharing portion of the meeting.

QUESTIONS FOR STEP REVIEW

Step One

We admitted we were powerless
over the effects of addiction,
that our lives had become unmanageable.

Step One forms the foundation for working the other steps. Admitting our powerlessness and accepting the unmanageability of our lives is not an easy thing to do. Although our behavior has caused us stress and pain, it is difficult to let go and trust that our lives can work out well. The idea that there are areas over which we are powerless is a new concept for us. It is much easier for us to feel that we have power and are in control.

• • •

In what area of your life do you experience the strongest need to be in control?

What are the consequences of your self-destructive habits?

What difficulties are you having in recognizing your powerlessness and your life's unmanageability?

What major event in your life has caused you to realize the extent of your pain?

Step Two

Came to believe that a power greater than
ourselves could restore us to sanity.

Step Two gives us new hope to see that help is available
to us if we simply reach out and accept what our Higher
Power has to offer. It is here that we form the foundation
for growth of our spiritual life, which helps us become the
person we want to be. What is required of us is a willingness
to believe that a power greater than ourselves is waiting
to help us. What follows as we proceed through the steps
is a process that brings our Higher Power into our lives
and enables us to grow in love, health, and grace.

• • •

List experiences that caused you to lose faith in God.

Have you mistakenly believed that it was your responsibility
to create faith yourself instead of accepting faith as a gift?
Explain.

What is keeping you from truly believing that a power greater
than yourself can restore you to sanity?

Describe your inability to manage your own affairs.

Step Three

Made a decision to turn our will and our lives over
to the care of God *as we understood God.*

Step Three is an affirmative step. It is time to make a
decision. In the first two steps, we became aware of our
condition and accepted the idea of a power greater than
ourselves. Although we are beginning to know and trust
God, we may find it difficult to think of allowing a Higher
Power to be totally in charge of our lives. However, if the
alternative is facing the loss of something critical to our
existence, our Higher Power's guidance may be easier to
accept.

· · ·

Which parts of your life are you willing to turn over to
your Higher Power?

Which parts of your life are you unwilling to turn over to
your Higher Power? What prevents you from giving them
up?

Why do you suppose that surrendering your life to a Higher
Power reduces the stress in your life?

What do you hope to experience as a result of your decision
to surrender to your Higher Power's will?

Step Four

Made a searching and fearless moral
inventory of ourselves.

Step Four is a tool to help us understand our current
behavior patterns and recognize our need for God's guidance in our lives. Here, we examine our behavior and expand
our understanding of ourselves. Being totally thorough and
honest in preparing our inventory helps us to see the obstacles that have prevented us from knowing ourselves and
acknowledging our deepest feelings about life.

. . .

What is your major strength? How does it support you?

What is your major weakness? How does it hurt you?

Which of your present behaviors is the most damaging to
your life? Explain.

In what areas of your life do you suspect that denial is at
work?

Step Five

Admitted to God, to ourselves, and to another human
being the exact nature of our wrongs.

Step Five requires that we engage in honest confrontations
with ourselves and others by admitting our faults to God,
to ourselves, and to another person. By doing so, we begin
to set aside our pride and see ourselves in true perspective.
We also realize how our growing relationship with our
Higher Power gives us the courage to examine ourselves,
accept who we are, and reveal our true selves. Step Five
helps us acknowledge and discard our old survival skills
and move toward a new and healthier life.

• • •

What can be gained by admitting your faults to another
person?

What is your resistance to sharing your story with another
person?

Which of your faults is the most difficult to acknowledge?
Why?

In what ways will admitting to God, to yourself, and to
another stop you from deceiving yourself?

Step Six

Were entirely ready to have God remove
all these defects of character.

The task of removing our ineffective behavior is more than we can handle alone. Step Six does not indicate that we do the removing; all we have to do is be "entirely ready" for it to happen. We can become ready by faithfully working the steps and being willing to let our Higher Power assist us in removing our shortcomings. The character traits we want to eliminate are often deeply ingrained patterns of behavior. They will not vanish overnight. We must be patient while our Higher Power is shaping us into new people. Allowing God be in control helps us to trust more completely.

. . .

What do you fear by having your character defects removed?

Identify two character defects you are not ready to have removed.

Why is it necessary to learn humility before your Higher Power can remove your defects of character?

What is interfering with your readiness to have God remove your shortcomings?

Step Seven
Humbly asked God to remove our shortcomings.

Humility is the central idea of Step Seven. By practicing humility we receive the strength necessary to work the steps and achieve satisfactory results. We recognize that a major portion of our lives has been devoted to fulfilling our self-centered desires. We must set aside these prideful, selfish behavior patterns and realize that humility frees our spirit. Step Seven requires surrendering our will to our Higher Power so that we may receive the serenity necessary to achieve the happiness we seek.

• • •

How are you benefiting from God's presence in your life?

What special blessings has your Higher Power sent to you since you began your Twelve-Step program of recovery?

List examples that indicate you are practicing humility.

Which of your negative character traits are becoming positive? Explain how this change is impacting your life.

173

Step Eight

Made a list of all persons we had harmed, and
became willing to make amends to them all.

Step Eight begins the process of healing damaged relationships through our willingness to make amends for
past misdeeds. We prepare ourselves to carry out our Higher
Power's master plan for our lives by preparing to make
amends. We can let go of our resentments and start to
overcome the guilt, the shame, and low self-esteem we have
acquired through our harmful actions. Through the gift
of the steps, we have the necessary tools to overcome these
damaging conditions and mend our broken friendships.

. . .

List three personal experiences that require making amends.

How will making amends help free you from resentment
and shame?

How does your unwillingness to forgive others block your
progress and hurt your relationship with your Higher Power?

Why is forgiving yourself an important factor in the amends-
making process?

Step Nine

Made direct amends to such people wherever possible, except when to do so would injure them or others.

Step Nine fulfills our requirement to reconcile with others. We clear our "garden" of dead leaves and "rake up and discard" the old habits. We face our faults, admit our wrongs, and ask for and extend forgiveness. Making amends will release us from many of the resentments of our past. It is a means of achieving serenity in our lives by seeking forgiveness from those we have harmed and making restitution where necessary.

· · ·

How will completing Step Nine enable you to bury the past and improve your self-esteem?

What difficulties are you having in making amends?

Who on your amends list causes you the most anxiety? What is the cause of this anxiety?

Who on your amends list do you consider to be an enemy? How do you plan to make this amend?

Step Ten

Continued to take personal inventory and, when we were wrong, promptly admitted it.

Step Ten points the way toward continued spiritual growth. We consciously examine our daily conduct and make adjustments where necessary. We look at ourselves, see our errors, promptly admit them, and make corrections. Taking regular inventory makes us more conscious of our strengths and weaknesses. We are less inclined to yield to feelings of loneliness, self-righteousness, and anger if we remain emotionally balanced and gather courage as we see our strengths increasing. We become more focused and capable of living the life we desire.

· · ·

List an example that shows you are relating better to others.

Cite a recent situation in which you did not behave appropriately. What did you do when you realized you were in error?

How does taking a daily inventory support your spiritual growth?

How does correcting your wrongs save you from unnecessary consequences?

Step Eleven

Sought through prayer and meditation to improve our
conscious contact with God *as we understood God,*
praying only for knowledge of God's will for us
and the power to carry that out.

To protect what we have learned, we must continually
seek to know our Higher Power's will for us. A daily regimen
of prayer and meditation makes it clear that relief is just
a day-to-day reprieve. Our approach to Step Eleven will
vary in intent and intensity; it indicates our commitment
to a prayerful life. If we are communicating with our Higher
Power, a feeling of joy will infuse our fellowship and friendship with others. We will reap rich benefits. Ideally, we
practice this step daily upon awakening and retiring, to
remind us that we must sincerely and humbly want God's
will for us.

• • •

Describe a situation where you delayed taking action because
you were "waiting" for God's will. What happened?

Cite an example in which your Higher Power answered
your prayers through another individual or a new experience.

What do you experience when quietly praying to God?

How has your life improved as a result of working the
steps?

Step Twelve

Having had a spiritual awakening as the result of these
steps, we tried to carry this message to others, and
to practice these principles in all our affairs.

Each of the Twelve Steps is a vital part of fulfilling our
Higher Power's plan for us. Conscientious attention to working the steps develops in us a level of love, acceptance,
honesty, and peace of mind unequalled at any other time
in our lives. Step Twelve invites us to promote our own
growth by helping others. Our willingness to share our
commitment to recovery and our growing awareness of our
Higher Power's presence in our lives keep us ever-vigilant
for ways to share our new confidence.

• • •

Cite an example that shows you are "living" the steps.

List a concern you had and describe your experience of
resolving it by applying the Twelve Steps.

What is your favorite way of "carrying the message" to others
in recovery?

How do you practice the principles of the steps in all your
affairs?

APPENDIX TWO

SELF-HELP RESOURCES

Adult Children of Alcoholics
Central Service Board
P.O. Box 3216
Torrance, California 90505
(310) 534-1815

Al-Anon/Alateen
Family Group Headquarters, Inc.
862 Midtown Station
New York, New York 10018
(212) 302-7240

Alcoholics Anonymous
World Services, Inc.
468 Park Avenue South
New York, New York 10016
(212) 686-1100

Co-Dependents Anonymous
P.O. Box 33577
Phoenix, Arizona 85067-3577
(602) 277-7991

Debtors Anonymous
P.O. Box 20322
New York, New York 10025-9992
(212) 642-8220

Emotions Anonymous
P.O. Box 4245
St. Paul, Minnesota 55104
(612) 647-9712

Gamblers Anonymous
P.O. Box 17173
Los Angeles, California 90017
(213) 386-8789

Narcotics Anonymous
P.O. Box 9999
Van Nuys, California 91406
(818) 780-3951

National Association for Children of Alcoholics
11426 Rockville Pike, Suite 100
Rockville, Maryland 20852
(301) 468-0985

Overeaters Anonymous World Service Office
2190 - 190th Street
Torrance, California 90504
(310) 618-8835

Sexaholics Anonymous
P.O. Box 300
Simi Valley, California 93062
(805) 581-3343

APPENDIX THREE

MILESTONES IN RECOVERY

- We feel comfortable with people, including authority figures.
- We have a strong identity and generally approve of ourselves.
- We accept and use personal criticism in a positive way.
- As we face our own life situation, we find we are attracted by strengths and understand the weaknesses in our relationships with other people.
- We are recovering through loving and focusing on ourselves; we accept responsibility for our own thoughts and actions.
- We feel comfortable standing up for ourselves when it is appropriate.
- We are enjoying peace and serenity, trusting that God is guiding our recovery.
- We love people who love and take care of themselves.
- We are free to feel and express our feelings even when they cause us pain.
- We have a healthy sense of self-esteem.
- We are developing new skills that allow us to initiate and complete ideas and projects.
- We take prudent action by first considering alternative behaviors and possible consequences.
- We rely more and more on God as our Higher Power.

PROMISES

If we are painstaking about this phase of our development, we will be amazed before we are half way through.

- We are going to know a new freedom and a new happiness.
- We will not regret the past nor wish to shut the door on it.
- We will comprehend the word serenity and we will know peace.
- No matter how far down the scale we have gone, we will see how our experience can benefit others.
- That feeling uf uselessness and self-pity will disappear.
- We will lose interest in selfish things and gain interest in our fellows.
- Self seeking will slip away.
- Our whole attitude and outlook upon life will change.
- Fear of people and of economic insecurity will leave us.
- We will intuitively know how to handle situations that used to baffle us.
- We will suddenly realize that God is doing for us what we could not do for ourselves.

Are these extravagant promises? We think not. They are being fulfilled among us—sometimes quickly, sometimes slowly. They will always materialize if we work for them.

COMMON BEHAVIOR CHARACTERISTICS

- We have feelings of low self-esteem that cause us to judge ourselves and others without mercy. We cover up or compensate by trying to be perfect, take responsibility for others, attempt to control the outcome of unpredictable events, get angry when things don't go our way, or gossip instead of confronting an issue.

- We tend to isolate ourselves and to feel uneasy around other people, especially authority figures.

- We are approval seekers and will do anything to make people like us. We are extremely loyal even in the face of evidence that suggests loyalty is undeserved.

- We are intimidated by angry people and personal criticism. This causes us to feel anxious and overly sensitive.

- We habitually choose to have relationships with emotionally unavailable people with addictive personalities. We are usually less attracted to healthy, caring people.

- We live life as victims and are attracted to other victims in our love and friendship relationships. We confuse love with pity and tend to "love" people we can pity and rescue.

- We are either overly responsible or very irresponsible. We try to solve others' problems or expect others to be responsible for us. This enables us to avoid looking closely at our own behavior.

- We feel guilty when we stand up for ourselves or act assertively. We give in to others instead of taking care of ourselves.

- We deny, minimize, or repress our feelings from our traumatic childhoods. We have difficulty expressing our feelings and are unaware of the impact this has on our lives.

- We are dependent personalities who are terrified of rejection or abandonment. We tend to stay in jobs or relationships that are harmful to us. Our fears can either stop us from ending hurtful relationships or prevent us from entering healthy, rewarding ones.

- Denial, isolation, control, and misplaced guilt are symptoms of family dysfunction. Because of these behaviors, we feel hopeless and helpless.

- We have difficulty with intimate relationships. We feel insecure and lack trust in others. We don't have clearly defined boundaries and become enmeshed with our partner's needs and emotions.

- We have difficulty following projects through from beginning to end.

- We have a strong need to be in control. We overreact to change over which we have no control.

- We tend to be impulsive. We take action before considering alternative behaviors or possible consequences.

THE TWELVE STEPS

1. We admitted we were powerless over the effects of addiction—that our lives had become unmanageable.

2. Came to believe that a Power greater than ourselves could restore us to sanity.

3. Made a decision to turn our will and our lives over to the care of God *as we understood God.*

4. Made a searching and fearless moral inventory of ourselves.

5. Admitted to God, to ourselves, and to another human being the exact nature of our wrongs.

6. Were entirely ready to have God remove all these defects of character.

7. Humbly asked God to remove our shortcomings.

8. Made a list of all persons we had harmed, and became willing to make amends to them all.

9. Made direct amends to such people wherever possible, except when to do so would injure them or others.

10. Continued to take personal inventory and when we were wrong promptly admitted it.

11. Sought through prayer and meditation to improve our conscious contact with God, *as we understood God,* praying only for knowledge of His will for us and the power to carry that out.

12. Having had a spiritual awakening as the result of these steps, we tried to carry this message to alcoholics, and to practice these principles in all our affairs.

"PRAYER OF SAINT FRANCIS OF ASSISI"

Lord, make me an instrument of your peace!
Where there is hatred—let me sow love
Where there is injury—pardon
Where there is doubt—faith
Where there is despair—hope
Where there is darkness—light
Where there is sadness—joy
O Divine Master, grant that I may not so much seek
To be consoled—as to console
To be loved—as to love
for
It is in giving—that we receive
It is in pardoning—that we are pardoned
It is in dying—that
we are born to eternal life.

Amen

SERENITY PRAYER

God, grant me the serenity
to accept the things
I cannot change,
the courage to change
the things I can,
and the wisdom
to know the difference.

Reinhold Niebuhr

For a complete list of books published by
RPI Publishing, you may write to:

RPI Publishing
P.O. Box 44
Curtis, WA 98538

(800) 873-8384